LOVING YOU AND LOOSING ME!

LOVING YOU AND LOOSING ME!

By Ervin Nubian Holloway

Published by

MIDNIGHT EXPRESS BOOKS

LOVING YOU AND LOOSING ME

ISBN-13: 978-0692279953
ISBN-10: 0692279954

Published by
MIDNIGHT EXPRESS BOOKS
POBox 69
Berryville AR 72616
(870) 210-3772
MEBooks1@yahoo.com

LOVING YOU AND LOOSING ME!

By Ervin Nubian Holloway

Foreword

This book is dedicated to the many women who I have shared, both lasting and unlasting memories with.

This book is also dedicated to every woman who may have had a personal relationship with one of these men mention within these pages.

I wrote this book for various reasons. Some are too personal for public criteria. However, I have inserted one true event in which I was the sole caused of a gentle woman's heartbreak on page four.

I have used the word re-lasting-ship oppose to relationship.

I feel a relationship should "last."

Enjoy!

ERVIN NUBIAN HOLLOWAY
AUTHOR & POET
CEO OF UNDERGROUND POETS

Table of Contents

THE FATHER FIGURE

What is man? According to Merriam-Webster's Collegiate Dictionary, man is:

Husband or lover; one possessing in high degree the qualities consider distinctive of manhood; and the quality or state of being manly.

However, Christian Science says that man is: the compound idea of infinite Spirit or the spiritual image and likeness of God.

Then you have the people in ancient Africa who say that man is: Montu/Muntu, God and man infused into one being.

And then you have "women" who say that man is: a dirty dog, a lying dog, a cheating dog and a no good dog.

So whether man is a husband, lover or God, excluding the dog, he is a set of qualities that defines him as being

1. Mental,
2. Physical, and
3. Spiritual.

And these three qualities or directives are the things women look for in a man.

The other qualities, that is subjectively hidden from the un- parallel feminine gender is, Amun. Amun is an African name that means hidden.

This hidden quality is the father figure women tend to gravitate towards; because it tends to establish a masculine affection, whereas, most men fail to exhibit.

What I'm trying to convey as it relates to Amun is, man is a well-accepted meaning, dressed in physical flesh, unseen in spiritual form as an idealization of her father being projected into someone whom she looks for guidance and protection in.

So unconsciously, or consciously, she desired the man who has similar, if not all traits that her father so secretly displays. I can both understand and overstand why.

A father is the "man" of the house. He commands authority in a warm compassionate way. He has a female chromosome of XY, X being the origin of his existence. He has strength. He leads in a way that reflects the approval of his female counterpart.

Therefore, these characteristics and more are what she humble herself during childhood. And these will be the same characteristics she goes toward during her adulthood when it comes to character traits of her daddy. And it's no strange reason why women today are referring to their "men" as Cake Daddy, Sugar Daddy, Lil' Daddy, or preferably just Daddy.

For just like "fathers," these 'daddies' make preparation to meet the required need of the woman. Or risk losing her.

Because normally, and notably. Women look for security in a man or a daddy. So in any woman eyes the daddy in the best investment a woman can have.

Care must be taken that these women are not look upon as gold-diggers base on their outlook for seeing men as security.

Women are naturally geared and raised to seek support in a male figure. So understandably, women will abbreviate their daddy in the guise of security, in the guise of bonds, in the guise of a future, in the guise of stocks, in the guise of dreams; but mainly, in the guise of a loving man that will protect her, provide for her and build for her, a foundation that is indiscriminately in tune with a decree of the:

Father Figure.

2

THE ONE FOR ME

He is the one for me.

Women typically use this phase because the man is usually sensitive, warm, fun, gentle, communicative, passionate, respectful, sensual, loving, supportive, sharing, non-argumentative, etc.

However, there is no texture in this phase. This category selection is use commonly among women as a standard of reference to the kind of man they want. As oppose to the kind of man they need.

What exactly is "The One For Me?"

Let's examine to find out.

Meet Monica; beautiful, independent, determine, smart, strong, and a bit over-zealous. She tells her friend Tangie, "Girl, I'm telling you, he's the one for me."

Tangie smacks her lips, ""How can you be so sure, Monica. You thought that about the last man and he drugged you through the mud."

Monica ignores her friend's warning and say, "All apples that fall from the tree aren't bad, Tangie."

"But," Tangie replies. "One apple can spoil the whole bunch."

This is unacceptable to Monica who believes that all men are not dogs. And there are "some" good men out there. Tangie however is not convinced. Especially, since the last man dogged her best friend.

Nevertheless, no matter what Tangie opinions are. They will not bare any impact on Monica's decision making policy as to how she feels about her own man.

Tangie must realize two things. 1) A woman feels incomplete without a man. 2) Women are emotional beings and they need someone to share their emotions with.

Tangie, being a woman should know this. But, Monica is too caught up in "The One For Me." That she fails to take notice that Tangie is consciously in love with her, thereby creating a wall between every good man Monica feel is:

The One For Me.

THE SUCCESSFUL MAN

Is well groomed. Dress casual. Articulate. Respectful. Drinks imported wine as oppose to cheap beer. Drive a Jag or Bentley traverse to a car with tinted windows, loud music, flashy rims, ridiculous paint jobs and hydraulics.

This successful man goes to ball-rooms gatherings, and never, never to unrelenting clubs.

He loves children, but care not to have one of his own. His life is spent mostly flying from state to state, and country to country. His communication and business transactions are usually taken care of by a sexy, twenty something year old secretary fresh out of college.

He loves his success. It is equivalent to commercial sex and atmospheric drugs. Which in turn, creates difficulties between him and Neon; a highly attractive reporter in the down town area of Atlanta.

One day while love sick and stressing, Neon, out of desperation calls her co-worker, Patricia. "Could you meet me at Piedmont Park?"

"What time?" Patricia asked.

"An hour after I finish up my last report for the nightly news."

"Ok." Patricia agrees.

Now, what possibly could Neon want to discuss with Patricia that she cannot discuss with her man? It cannot possibly be about love. Because if it was love that made Neon and her man's relationship work in the beginning, it would have to be love that makes their relastingship work in the end.

"Thank you for coming," Neon says to Patricia.

"Girl you don't have to thank me. I know if the tables were turned you'll do the same thing for me. So what's up?" Patricia inquired while they walked.

"It's Darryle." Neon pouts.

"He isn't hitting or cheating on you?" Patricia voice sound alarming.

I would like to intermit a minute before Patricia continued. I wanna know why hitting & cheating are the most frequently asked questions by women when they think their girlfriends are going through a set of problems that are emotional and circumstantial. Could it be that "most" women do not completely trust men? I don't have any suitable conclusion to draw upon. However, I will say this. Mental abuse of a woman is just as worse than physical abuse of a woman.

Now back to, Patricia. "Because if he is, you better call nine-one-one or pour hot grits on his azz."

"Stop it, Patricia. You know Darryle would never do anything like that. He wouldn't hurt a fly. Besides," Neon unzipped her Gucci purse, "I stay strapped."

"Then what is it?"Patricia asked, though seeming unfazed by the Glock-40 that Neon displayed. "Darryle is everything a woman wants. He's successful and..."

"That's just it," Neon speaks with sadness in her voice while cutting Patricia short.

"That's just it!" Patricia declared. "I know you didn't bring me all the way down here because you're unhappy that your man is successful. Please don't tell me you did?"

"Yes." Neon sadness turns into watery eyes. "I'm sorry I brought you all the way down here for this. But his success is ruining our relationship. He's always working and never at home. And when he is home, it's twelve or one in the morning. I have a hectic schedule as it is. So it's impossible for me to see him."

Patricia snaps. "Girl, you are one ungrateful, sick bitch. I don't understand women like you."

"Women like me?" Neon fought hard to hold back tears.

"Yeah, women like you. Whether you're with the right man, the perfect man, a good man, a descent man or even a godly man; you all are not satisfied. You should be happy you gotta man."

"I thought you wanted me to be happy."

"I do. But not in a way that affects my own happiness, Neon. You have a man when most women don't. And you have a man that most women want. There is a lot of competition out there. Incarceration is one of them. Meaning, black men are being locked up at alarming rates. Inter-racial marriage is on the rise seventy percent more than it was ten years ago. Also meaning, there are less black men for the average black woman. And let's not forget all the college girls, church girls, hoochie mamas, strippers and gays you have to compete with. And you have the got-damn nerve to complain. Bye, Neon."

Let's analyzed Patricia snappy attitude to see if the situation is approachable.

For starters, I can overstand why Patricia snapped. However, I don't deem it appropriate. Neon is seriously in love with this man and came seeking sound advice from a person whom she considers to be her friend. Although, Patricia cites measurable facts as it relates to those who Neon has to compete with.

Nevertheless, Neon came seeking advice. Not the snappiness of Patricia impetuous attitude. Instead of endorsing a means by which Neon could yield a promising outcome with her man, Patricia has caused more uncertainty.

Patricia would have been more productive by implying that Neon find other objectives to be with her man, like changing her work hours, taking annual sick leaves, take longer vacations when she has put in over time or, since

Neon man is successful, take the secretary position so she can spend more time with her man.

This problem concerning Neon and her man success can easily be decimated…or any woman who find themselves in similar situations, as that of Neon.

The problem is women fail to do four critical things:

1. Listen to their inner-voice
2. Map out the problem
3. Find the solution
4. And stop letting their heart and friends make relationship-base decisions they know they are mentally capable of making.

THE THUGG

Conservative women call him "Bad Boy." Meaning, they want a man with a pinch of "Bad Boy" inside him. Skeptics would say this is conservative women way of surga-coating the word "Thug" so it can be sociably accepted.

I have no problem with conservative women connotation of the word. Whatever float their boats is fine with me.

Yet, I will say this. Why are conservative women and unconservative women attractive to "The Thugg?"

The answer is clear, women hate boredom. So a thug affords them a realistic amount of excitement and a bit of danger in a serious, yet protecting, threatening, kind of way. Anyway, we are well aware that science teaches us that opposite attracts. Being such, "The Thug" is the next best secret women of all ages and groups long to have by their side.

But, are these thugs accepted by these women family, friends and the community? Let's examine to see.

Meet Debra, a company manager, makes over two-hundred grand a year, works out excessively, and speaks several different languages. Her beauty, I would say, is average. She helps the poor and needy. Is a voice for the Black Community. And the list goes on and on…until she meets Ray Ray.

A 6'3", physical fit, gorgeous hunk of a man who has two problems. 1. Despite how angelic he is on the outside, it doesn't hide the demons brewing on the inside; and 2) Ray Ray is married to the streets.

Debra's family, friends and the community are aware of her thug-out boyfriend's way of life. And therefore, tries constantly to persuade Debra to pull away from "The Thug" before unrelated circumstances occur. Because to Debra's family, friends and community. He doesn't fit well with her public demeanor or her recognizable standards.

"Hi Debra." A few members of her family, friends and elders of the community speak in unison over the crowded gathering.

Debra greets them all politely and respectfully. "Hi you all."

"We were wondering could we have a moment with you." One of the community elders asked.

"Could it wait? I have so many people to attend to today. I don't want to disappoint all the people who gathered here to commemorate this special event."

"It will only take a minute," the community elder replies.

Debra looked around. See that the people who gather there today were enjoying themselves. "Ok, shoot. But only a minute though."

"We want to discuss matters concerning your boyfriend."

"My boy friend," Debra question. "Is there something wrong?"

"Only that his life style is predatory and dangerous." The community elder voiced his concerns.

With a stern attitude Debra replies, "You know nothing of my boyfriend's life style!"

"All you have to do is open your eyes and not be blinded by love and see what he's doing to the black community. While you're trying to alleviate the black community into reconstruction, he is trying to aggravate the black community into destruction. Two opposing forces heading in opposite directions, yet, only one can win."

"How dare you talk to me like that!" Debra's attitude becomes sterner.

"Watch your attitude, young lady," Debra's mother cuts in.

"Mother, don't tell me you are in on this to? Out of all people, I thought you would be the one to support me."

"Not when the man you love doesn't share the same vision for a productive future as you do."

"He is productive for me, mother. And that's all that matters right now in my life."

"And what about the life of others?" Debra's mother asked.

"The life of others!" Debra exclaimed. "Have I not given my life to others? Have I not sacrificed enough? I'm not a stray cat, mother. I don't have nine lives. At some point I have to have a life of my own. A life not always shared with family, friends and the community. But a life shared sometimes with my man. I hope you all can understand that. I must go now, bye."

Poor Debra. But she is not alone in this world inhabited by contingency-takeovers and thug-passion men.

Women daily are engulfed by this epidemic of thugs. Especially, when the ingredients like:

¼ street ambition

2/3 business savvy

A dash of compassion

A spoon of both rough and gentle sex

A cup of faith

And 4 inches of slippery tongue are mixed properly together.

Debra's family, friends and the community are unable to understand this. They fail to realize that Debra has a private life. A life that is not open or dictated by them. Debra also feels she did not come into the scheme of things, family, friends and community, to share her private life with them.

Therefore, instead of passing judgment, the family, friends and community, should have implied to Debra that she teach her man a more constructive or legal way to acquire money.

This approach would have placed Debra in a position to use the same intellectual faculties and skills, by which she became company manager to effectuate a change in her man economic and thug out life style.

Since the family, friends and community passed judgment, thus being ineffective in their approach. Debra future with "The Thug" may progress into an artificial relationship or incarceration for the both of them.

THE PLAYER

Has a realizable amount of women.

Smooth in every since of the word.

Wears the hottest and latest gear.

Slick talker.

Cunning.

Good looking.

Up on his game.

Elusive.

Open minded.

Both book and street smart.

Has an uncontrollable sex drive.

This is the man women claim there is something about him that make him so irresistible. But not the man they would trust or fall in love with.

What will happen when a woman falls in love with "The Playa?" Let's examine to find out.

Meet Daphne. A beauty salon owner; age twenty-five, not pretty but not ugly either. What she doesn't have in looks is made up in her banging body and endearing personality. One thing though, Daphne is unaware that her boyfriend is a playa. So she receives a call from her cousin Meka.

"Hey, what's up?" Daphne yawns over the phone.

"Chile, guess who I seen creeping last night?"

"Not your brother-in-law again. Your sister will have a fit if you ever decide to tell her, Meka."

"It's not my brother-in-law who was the one creeping," Meka spoke. "It's your man who was."

"What!" Daphne blurted out.

"I'm sorry, Daphne. But I had to tell you."

"Where did you see his azz at so I can catch him lying?"

"Coming out the Hilton. Do you want me to handle this with you, Daphne?"

"Appreciate it. But I'll take care of this on my own." Daphne hung up and called Tony.

"Hello." Tony answered.

"Bastard, where were you last night?" Daphne screams through the phone.

"First of all, don't be calling me raising your voice. Now what the hell did you say?"

"Bastard, you heard me the first time. So tell me where were you last night? Cuz Meka told me she seen you coming out the Hilton."

"Hold for a sec." Tony says and then makes the three way call with Meka.

"Hello," Meka picks up on the first ring.

"What the hell did you tell Daphne?" Tony growled.

14

"That your azz was out hoe-hopping."

"Now what do you have to say for yourself?" Daphne demanded an answer.

"Not a damn thang. You have made up your mind to believe Meka anyway. However, if Meka would have look closer to who I was with, she would have realized it was my cousin."

"I didn't know."

"I'm sure you didn't." Tony interrupted her. "Because you're always jumping to conclusions. But you and Meka can kiss my black azz."

<<<CLICK>>>.

Another relationship gone sour based on the assumption of Tony's alleged infidelity.

Here, Meka thought or "assumed" she was looking out for the well being of Daphne. Somehow Meka seemed to forget that Daphne is madly in love with "The Playa." And no matter what she tells Daphne concerning him, she will not believe as long as "The Playa" has a legitimate excuse.

Men are sacred to women, and vise-versa. So when a woman loves, she loves hard. The scope of Meka's assumption, without any concrete proof, then becomes irrelevant.

Meka should have known this since she was the one creeping with Daphne's man in the first place.

Ervin Nubian Holloway

THE RELIGIOUS MAN

Is MECHANICALLY indifferent to the physical FACULTIES of a woman.

me-chan-i-cal-ly

adj: caused by, resulting from, or relating to a process that involves a purely physical as opposed to a chemical or biological change or process.

fac-ul-ties

noun: an inherent capability, power or function. Any of the power of the mind formerly held by psychologist to form a basis for the explanation of all mental phenomena.

The religious man being mechanically indifferent to the physical faculties of a woman, prematurely thinks, that the applications of 'his' religious concepts should not be a process involving the purely physical needs of a woman. It should, as he thinks, involve the religious needs of him and him "only." So much so, that without conscious reasoning, he fails to provide her with the attention she continuously need.

And though I stated on the previous pages that women are emotional beings and they need someone to share those emotions with. I must state here that women need and love attention also.

And if the attention she require is not giving to her physical needs. Any regards to her religious needs that are not equally balance with her physical needs - will eventually become radioactive - thus resulting in disorder or chaos in violation of the laws of Ma'at.

But, if you want a better understanding of what is taking place between the Religious Man. You must first have an overstanding of what Ne'Osha is going through.

Sunday morning church is where Ne'Osha and Tammie decided to discuss her problems.

"Do you think it's a good time to have this conversation while the pastor is giving his sermon? You know in 1954 Dr. King accepted his first pastorate at this same Baptist church; a church with a well-educated congregation that had been led by minister Vernon Johnson who had protested against segregation."

"Don't lecture me, Tammie. I know the history of Dexter Avenue Baptist Church in its entirety. I was born right here in Montgomery, Alabama. Besides, you are kin to me, not the pastor. And blood is thicker than holy water."

Tammie laughed. "Girl, you are something else. Now, tell me what is going on. And don't beat around the bush."

"I have a man who is so religious that he is failing to provide me with the necessary attention. There you have it. No beating around the bush."

"Ok then. I will tell you this. You must learn there are three things men will place first in giving their undivided attention. First is their mother, who they unconsciously put before God. Second is their religion, that they put before women. Third is their sports that they place before their X-chromosome. Because testosterone has the ability to alienate estrogen levels that are correlated phenomena to the female physical makeup."

"Did I not tell you to lecture me, Tammie?"

I'm not lecturing you, Ne'Osha. I'm giving it to you raw and uncut. Religion is a touchy subject. A subject that has divided families. Nations. Caused wars. The shedding of blood. And the taken of lives. Religion is just too powerful for him to provide you with your physical needs. When providing you with religious needs is the "only" thing he want to provide you with."

"I don't have a problem with him providing me with religious needs, Tammie. But I want him to realize that it takes the trinity of

18

Mind/Body/And Soul; just as it takes the trinity of Father/Son/and the Holy Spirit to bring balance and harmony between the two."

Tammie crossed her legs, looked Ne'Osha in the eyes. "All that sounds good. But the outcome for him is already determined. I'm surprise you two made it this far. Since the both of you have different opposing belief systems. I have to go now. Call me later, ok."

Either Ne'Osha man is part of the problem or part of the solution. And Tammie's contradictory doubleness has made the matter more problematic than it needs to without a detail examination or analogy.

anal-o-gy

noun: inference that if two or more things agree with one another in some respect they will probably agree in other.

The above definition implies that Ne'Osha and her man can "agree to disagree" when religious indifferences are predicates for disparities. There can be mutual respect when different religions are involve.

But, Ne'Osha must be firm, yet lady like in building a relastingship that doesn't conflict with his religion. For there are ways in working around things just as there are ways in working things out. But more importantly, there are ways in working things together.

Because a working relationship, works well, when it works in the interest of mind/body/and soul; and not just in religious approximation, where he approximate just how much attention to give to Ne'Osha.

Ervin Nubian Holloway

THE INCARCERATED MAN

I decided to give the reader an insight into my own personal experience of being an incarcerated man.

I must state: the prison culture is very challenging and metallic. And to properly rehabilitate yourself is left solely up to you. The availability is there, books, trades, aerobics, social skills, designated as educational tools to combat recidivism, accumulate wealth legally and to use as an additive to protect against mental spoilage, physical decay, and society's compound statistics that you will be a product of your environment as oppose to being productive for your environment.

Yet, with adequate preparation, I vowed to never again be counted as a statistic. Now I overstand why an incarcerated man receives a number the moment he is culturally incarcerated. (Statistics are base on numbers.) And mine number was #10201-002.

The fabric on incarceration began for me over fifteen years ago. And during that time or I would say at the height of my development. My one on one experience with a female correctional officer led me to the overstanding why women are attracted to the Incarcerated Man.

I will not mention her real name for the sake of jeopardizing her job. So I will make up a name and call her, Najee. How I became intimate with Najee was something I had not plan. Nor had I taking any notice.

Who had noticed was a roommate of mine. He said she had smiled at me incriptively. I said to him that smiling was natural due to the fact women have an innate ability of using non-verbal expressions to say I am approachable - but do not get to close.

My roommate gave me a look that indicated I was either slow or I needed to break in a school house because I was just that dumb.

After careful consideration, I decided to test my roommate hypothesis.

hy-poth-e-sis

noun: a tentative assumption made in order to draw out and
test its logical or empirical consequences.

The very first test I did was to create a situation where I could compliment
her on a regular basis when no one was around. The compliments proved to
be highly effective. At times I would say, "Najee, you look radiant this
morning." She would smile briefly and tell me my compliment were stand-
ardly inappropriate. When she didn't report my compliments to her supervi-
sors, I knew it was time to legislate a series of compliments to reach my
objective. I did, and the smile on Najee's face was no longer brief. But
rather, a harmonic tone of contingence joy.

I want to point the reader to a book call METU NETER VOL-1, written by
scholar Ra Un Nefer Amen. In this METU NETER book he states:

*"in whatever way they have define it, whether they have articulate their view of it or not,
underlying all human endeavors is the quest for happiness."*

Due to the fact I was consciously aware of this by reading the METU
NETER, I became more adapt in my overstanding as to why women are
attracted to incarcerated men. I felt happiness was one part of the equation.
While fantasy made up the rest. For starters, when a woman isn't happy, she
creates antibodies from a mental stand point that ultimately combat her
unhappiness. She is not a "being" that deals well with the concepts of
feeling sad, down, or depressed. She is far too delicate for such emotional
difficulties.

Yet, the only way she can alleviate such difficulties is by replacing the man
who makes her unhappy with the man that makes her happy. The only man
who came close to bringing her joy is the "incarcerated man." At that
particular time, I happened to be an incarcerated man who constituted the
full meaning of Najee's happiness. And likewise, she constituted the full
meaning of my happiness. So much so that while Najee worked from

12:00am - 8:00am we engaged in a network of conversation coupled with moments of intense intimacy.

Regrettably for me, what me and Najee had going on was about to change due controlling to, a conversation I overheard her having with a co-worker.

"Hey Najee, girl. What's the latest with you and that Nubian guy? I notice you've been smiling a lot."

"Everything is ok, I guess; since it was your idea for me to get with him in the first place."

"My idea?" The coworker question.

"Yes, your idea. You indicated that I should find someone who is incarcerated, a man who will make me happy. Say sweet and strength words to me. You also mentioned how you had been intimate with an incarcerated man for four years with a four year old child who you claim is your husband's child."

"Come on, Najee. You know the situation between me and my husband. He has become lazy as hell. He doesn't work. Sex is boring. We're constantly arguing. And mind you. These arguments are started by him. Which means two things - he's either screwing some woman in our house while I'm at work or he's planning a divorce. And my husband is the kind of man who throws the rock but hides his hand."

"That might be true, and I understand what you're saying, but two wrongs don't make it right."

The coworker looked herself over, then dabbed a little makeup onto her face realizing for the first time in her life that an incarcerated man had restored her to a better, higher, or more worthy state and said "Yea, but it damn sho make it even."

The following day I expressed my unwillingness to Najee. I told her that we should end our relationship in return for a relastingship. I explained it was the best choice for the both of us. That having a relationship with an incarcerated man isn't realistically attainable. There's the possibility of her losing her job and thus being brought under heavy scrutiny. That besides the "college girl and the professor," or the "nurse and the patient," or the "pool boy and the lonely wife," or the "secretary and the boss." The *incarcerated man and the female correctional officer* top the list of the ultimate fantasy.

I then concluded by telling Najee. She needed to go back to her man to determine what caused her unhappiness. Try to resolve or fix the problem in order to bring joy back into her life. And do not be blind by the 'peaches and cream' scenario whereas there will be no problems in a relationship because problems are like ATOMS - they are the building blocks of a relationship "only" if you let them MATTER.

For life at times can be disingenuous with problems. There are problems on the job. Problems with the environment. Problems that you take to prayer so that God may work them out for you. Problems with your family. Problems with your health. Problems! Problems! Problems!

The only good thing about problems is, they are workable and solvable. If you can't work through the problem, work around them. If you can't work around them, work between them. If you can't work between them, work over them. And if you can't work over them, find a working solution that works for you.

THE PERFECT MAN & THE GOOD MAN

I ask women this often. Which would they rather have, a perfect man or a good man?

The answers are always intellectually light or predictable. The first woman I ever asked was my daughter, Diamond; the love of my life and the sum of my existence.

Her reply was, "I would rather have a good man. Because ain't no man perfect."

Does my daughter's 'answer' contradict the statement women make when they say: "Good men are hard to find."

Where is the intelligence of choosing a Good Man over a Perfect Man if: "Good men are hard to find?"

Is not JUST having a man good enough? Is not having a man that is perfect for you, good enough? Or, is being good enough, just isn't good enough?

My stance is: A good man will always be 'just' a "good man." He will never rise above the standards of a Good Man or live out to see his true perfectionism because he simply stays a good man.

Per-fec-tion-ism

noun: the doctrine that the perfection of moral character constitute a person *highest good*.

It can now be said that a perfect man constitute a Good Man, or a person *highest good*.

To me, women are the most highly evolve beings on this planet; perfect in every sense of the word. But they have to let go of the notion that a perfect man is unattainable. And choosing a Perfect Man implies the desire not to conform to established rules trademarked by society's conflicting interest of choosing a Good Man over a Perfect Man, when in fact, a Good Man is always commonly chosen not to be in opposition with society's conflicting interest. To avoid any conflict, she advocates the concept of choosing a Good Man over a Perfect Man because, to her, the only man that is perfect is *the man upstairs*.

Whether *the man upstairs* implies the perfect man she imagines in her mind, (mind and heaven are synonymous with each other.) It becomes a clear indication that she only recognizes a Supernatural Being as perfect and not man. This becomes conflicting in of itself (only recognizing a Supernatural Being as perfect,) because she regularly refers to God in the context of a man. As if God and Man are somehow *interchangeable*.

in-ter-change-able

adj: permitting mutual substitution. To put each of the two things in the *place of the other*.

Does the definition above illustrate why women use God and Man interchangeably? Let me explain.

In her IMAGINATION, God is the Perfect Man. And the "only" man who is perfect, is *the Man upstairs*. So she wants a man that is perfect like *the Man upstairs*. So she tries to SUBSTITUTE the TWO, (God and Man.) in the place of the other.

Unfortunately since God is submerge in her consciousness as a Supernatural Being. The concept of choosing a "man" becomes irrelevant because he is not a Supernatural Being nor is he perfect. Therefore, the Perfect Man becomes obsolete and the Good Man is chosen. Because the Good Man is:

- Good to her
- Good for her
- Do Good by her

- And make Good love to her.

So a Good Man is all she need because a Perfect Man is not realistically attainable.

Although the "Good Man" and the "Perfect Man" may be slightly different, a woman doesn't need a man who is different – but a man that makes a difference.

Ervin Nubian Holloway

THE PARTYING MAN

This is all he does, party. Not only does he party. He parties hard.

He is at every event enjoying the social gathering and all the entertainment that comes with it.

The nightlife may be superficial to some. To him it is leisurely up-lifting and emotionally therapeutic.

Yet, in comes Tara who has became grammatical by using successive phases, (being sassy) against her fiancé's nightlife of partying. Irrespective of the fact, the club is where Tara met him in the first place.

Tara, text messages her friend Rick, who by the way, is attracted to men only and goes by the name of Rickie.

Rickie returned the text message explaining he was at the Montgomery Federal Court House testifying against a government informant - who is giving false testimony on his nephew, Ray Ray and to meet him at the airport in fifteen minutes.

Tara arrived at the airport, late as usual. The look on Rickie's face showed he was mad as hell.

"Sorry I'm late." Tara said apologetically.

"Black heifer, I should go ham on your azz. You know I have a plane to catch. The feds gonna be all over my azz since my testimony help freed Ray Ray and the rest of his crew of embellish thugs."

"But, you haven't done anything wrong, Rickie. Giving testimony in the defense of your nephew is not criminal."

"You're right. But possible jury tampering and owing the IRS two million in back taxes is."

"So why not just pay the money instead of leaving the country?"

"Are you crazy, Tara? The only thing the IRS will get from me is a role of stained toilet paper because I ain't giving them shit. Anyway, I'm using the two million to get my sex changed."

Tara tried not to laugh and said, "A two million dollar coochie comes with an insurance policy and a safe deposit box I hope."

"Girl, and credit cards too." Rickie returned the laugh. "So tell me what's bothering you."

"My fiancé is letting his habit of partying take precedent over our relationship."

"Is he spending any time with you?"

"Yes, I guess."

"Then there's no problem."

"Did you not hear me, Rickie. I said my fiancé partying is taking precedent over our relationship."

"I heard you. But you're not listening. If a man is spending time with you, no matter how much he is partying, it shouldn't matter as long as he's still with you. Unless you're insecure about something, Tara."

"Insecure about what?" Tara exclaimed.

"That your fiancé will likely meet other prospects the way he met you. That this irritates the hell out of you because you're not confident in your fiancé ability to remain faithful to you."

"How did you come to this conclusion, Mr. Specialist on women insecurities?"

"I might be gay, Tara, but I'm still a man who knows how to recognize signs of insecurities."

<intercom> Flight 198 heading for Cuba is boarding.

"That's my flight, gotta go. Take care, Tara."

"I will." Tara said giving her friend a long hug then moments later, exiting the airport without a clear and definite answer.

Tell me, what did Tara expect from Rickie? I know she wanted an answer or a solution.

Nevertheless, Tara's circumstances are not unusual. And, in fact, can be traceable, not to her insecurities as Rickie suggested but to the fact that all she needs to do is communicate with her fiancé concerning his habit of partying.

Communication doesn't involve an invalid or unenforceable method. It involves the act of conversation or discourse to cultivate and harness information, by expressing the exchange of ideas through productive discussing to reach a desire result.

Tara's desire is to bring her fiancé's habit of being a party animal under some kind of control. Basically, she is trying to domesticate him into a non-partying life style where quality time take precedent over their relationship.

In order for this to occur, Tara must verbally articulate a meaningful dialogue that won't create any language barriers.

Sadly, Tara is the one who is creating the barriers. And anything meaningful becomes even bigger problems for Tara and her partying man.

Ervin Nubian Holloway

THE ABUSIVE MAN

He's the one who will hit a woman but is afraid to hit a man. He will degrade his woman but does not want another man to degrade his mother, sister, aunt, niece or female cousins.

At times he is very vex; lacks a sense of direction. He has a gothic attitude. He is insecure about his embellish masculinity. And the list goes on and on.

This man, well I will not call him a man. This thing does not value the vaulting nature or the sacredness of a woman. His abusiveness will create sizable amounts of damage upon a woman's physical and mental realities. So damaging, that she may equate physical abuse with love in the guise of discipline, the way a parent does when punishing a child for misbehaving.

For this very reason of abuse by "The Abusive Man," you must meet Kiyah.

Although Kiyah graphically explained I should keep her story a secret, I assured her on one condition. That she give me the name of the man that is abusing her.

I dropped the letter in the mail-box for Kiyah response.

A week later Kiyah wrote back with these words:

> Dear Ervin:
>
> I know you mean well. But he will kill me if I tell anyone. Anyway, what will it change? The scars will still be emotionally and physically a part of me. The young innocence I once felt has now become incomplete. It matters little if I'll ever be whole again.

It matters little which direction I choose to travel in this abuse. The roads will be rough, anyhow. Am just hoping this road will hurry up and lead to a dead end.

You asked me in your letter to accept your "one condition." But, your "one condition" doesn't ensure my safety. You might say, "But Kiyah, you're not safe now." You're so right. But being not safe is better than being dead.

See, you must understand that I'm so scared of him. It's not the normal scare shown in the big Hollywood movies where horror flicks meet the big screens. It's the scare, shown in the eyes of a predator. A predator that has me waking up in the middle of the night screaming. No one hear my cries.

No knight in shining armor. No super hero sketched across comic books. No handsome prince told in the Sleeping Beauty Stories. Then I'm reminded to call on God. But sadly, he never answers. Maybe because, he's scared and needs saving too.

Yours Truly,
Kiyah.

PS... keep me in your prayers.

As oppose to writing Kiyah a letter. I decided to write her this poem:

Don't get in confuse
A relationship isn't base on abuse
So why do you let him beat you
Mentally he should find a way to teach you
Instead of using his hand to reach you
And tell me,
How is it,
You who gave birth to man
Will continue to let him raise his hand
To strike you
Here's some advice to you

Because there's no telling what he might do
In a abusive situation
Where the evolution of one problem
Or the solution of another
Eventually brings back the first problem
That gave rise to the other.

I dropped the "poem" in the mail-box and waited on a response. Days went by without a response from Kiyah.

After a few months, I went about my normal routine. Reading, exercising, watching my favorite news station, CNN; and taking a few classes. You know to prepare myself for the outside world. Because being incarcerated in a federal prison can either make you or break you, and I'd rather be broke and free than to be broke and locked up. Therefore, I was going to seize every opportunity learning the ins and outs of economics.

During the mist of my learning, I begin to worry about Kiyah. I couldn't call her. The contact I had was through mail only. I figure something had to be wrong. This wasn't like her not to write back.

And then, in a sudden flash! It dawned on me. Kiyah wasn't being abuse physically but sexually. And the abuse wasn't cause by a boy-friend but by her step-father.

"How could I have been so stupid?" I thought to myself. I should have known when she said:

> "Ervin I'm so scared of him. It's not the normal scare
> shown in horror movies. But the scare shown in the eyes of
> a predator."

And the sad thing is, Kiyah was in her teens. For most adult men are seen as *predators* and trespassers in the lives of a child who haven't reach the require legal age.

Shortly after, I immediately notified the Montgomery Police Department. I gave them Kiyah's address and informed them that I felt a young girl was being sexually abuse by her step-father.

Three days later at approximately 2:00pm, I was told to appear at the visitation room.

When I got there, two white detectives of medium built, one with hunting eyes, were waiting patiently on my arrival.

"Have a seat," the detective with hunting eyes said.

I sat down cautiously while making direct eye contact.

The other medium built officer watched me closely and began taking down notes.

"I am Detective Balwin. The detective with the note pad is Detective Bevins. I will cut the small talk. Do you know why we are here?"

I shook my shoulders up and down indicating I didn't have the slightest clue.

"You called our office reporting a crime of sexual abuse, didn't you?"

"I had. But that was three days ago. You guys sure work fast."

"We checked into your story right away."

"Glad to hear that you did. So that means an arrest was made?"

"Sorry, but no." The detective said. "The address you gave was of an old abandon house. Are you sure you had the right address?"

"I'm more than sure. For Christ sake, she wrote me twice! I wrote twice also. When I didn't get a response! I called you guys."

There was a deep silence. I could sense something wasn't right. These two chumps were holding out on me. "Ok," I said breaking the silence. "Tell me what's going on?"

"Here's what we know. A young girl three years ago lived in the house you were writing to. I was the one initially doing the investigation until I brought my partner along. Felt really bad I couldn't put her step-father away. But without Kiyah's testimony, we had no case."

I jumped from my seat angrily, "You mean to tell me you sack of shits knew and no arrest was made."

"Calm down young man."

"Nah, you calm the fuck down. I'm going back to my dormitory."

"Don't you wanna hear what happen to Kiyah?"

I paused, thought about it for a moment, then immediately turned back around and sat back down. "Go ahead." I informed him.

"After many failed attempts to persuade Kiyah to testify, my partner decided it was best we closed the case. I, however, continue to drive by Kiyah's house."

"That's all you did?" I said more angry than I was before.

"What more could I do?" The detective said in a hopeless tone.

"Sorry excuse for an officer." I blatantly said.

Fed up with the way I was talking to his partner, Detective Bevins ran up on me violently and grabbed me by the neck of my collar and said, "Listen you sack of black shit. There was a nine-one-one call placed by a next door neighbor saying she heard gun shots. When my partner got to the scene, two bodies were laying on the floor."

I pulled the detective hands from my collar and pushed him off me. "What the hell are you talking about?"

"Idiot! The girl wracked her step-father then herself."

I peered into his blue eyes. "Then who was it writing me all those times?"

"We were hoping you could tell us." He answered.

"You two cops are sick. Move out my got-damn way!" I pushed between them both and made my way toward the dormitory to get some sleep.

I awaken the next morning playing out the whole event transcribed between me and the detectives. I knew four things:

1. I had placed an ad with a Pen Pal service that prohibits minors from writing.
2. That was three years ago.
3. Somehow without being detected by the Pen Pal service, Kiyah got the ad and start writing me. And,
4. She was crying out for help.

I had to rethink everything over again. This girl was dead when she was writing me. Even the officers bore witness to her death. I have heard people say that they have seen ghosts and spirits. Yet, none said that ghosts or spirits wrote them letters. There had to be a logical explanation for all this.

I GOT IT!

I ran out the dormitory toward the Correctional Officers' main office. Threw Kiyah's letters on the desk and said, "Could you explain this?"

"Explain what, Mr. Holloway?" A female correctional officer with a mouth-watering body asked.

I pointed at the date marked by the Post Office and rudely said, "Don't play fucking games with me. You know what the fuck I'm talking about. Somebody up in this office has been holding my mail. And I want some got-damn answers!"

Her scary azz hit the alarm button. In came the Captain, the Lieutenant, beat-down-crew and a host of other correctional officers too numerous to count.

"If it isn't Mr. Holloway. What is it now?" The sound of the Captain voice was a sure sign he was tired of my shit.

"These letters got to me three years later. And I wanna know why?"

"This is what all the fuss is about? To ease some of your frustration, Mr. Holloway, I will inform you of this. We had to hold your mail because of the vast amount you were receiving. We have to make sure Federal Policy is carried out as it relates to inmates mail. I hope this address your problem."

Pissed, I got within arm reach of the Captain and swung. In minutes the beat-down-crew was all over me. I could feel boots in my ribs, elbows in my back and a magnitude of blows pounding against my face. With blood oozing from my lips and nose, I manage to say these words, "If I would have gotten these letters three years ago, I could have saved the life of a sexually abused child."

After explaining the situation to the Captain, he agreed not to press charges. However, I was still placed in solitary confinement where I decided to write this book. I felt I owed it to Kiyah that her story be told. Hope the reader find something meaningful and heart touching in what I have written.

Keep the faith.

Ervin Nubian Holloway

Ervin Nubian Holloway

THE FAITHFUL MAN

Have you ever loved someone more than you love life, God, family or even yourself?

Well, I have. Yet, loving her so much was producing an unusual set of circumstances inside of me that left within my mist a loneliness which seem to occupy my own existence.

See, when you love someone. It seems magical. A spell, sorcery or enchantment, capable of inspiring a false sense of security and eternity infused in one. What I mean by false sense is: I assumed all the feelings and emotions I invested were a driving point that would lead me to a road filled with eternity, filled with directions, filled with travel plans, filled with instructions, filled with a manual, but most of all, filled with a sense where I needed her more than a Christian need Jesus/Heru, a Muslim need Allah, and a missing child needs his or her parents.

Basically, I needed her to love me the way I loved her.

However, this was the first mistake I made. Thinking she could realistically love me the way I loved her.

I had to learn that no two loves are the same and won't afford each other their basic emotional needs. A man's love may be strong, aggressive, unknowing, cryptic, misleading, narrow, undetected, escapable, gripping, risky, stagnant, isolated, intense, coerce, un-poetic, graphic or dreamy.

While a woman's love maybe passionate, sweet, unlimited, warm, immortal, venerating, welcoming, emotional, gentle, unavoidable, or poetry in its feminine form.

Since woman and man were created for each other, I determined that two loves can be the same with 1) hard work, 2) effort, and 3) dedication.

And I decided to provide an avenue base on these three things that will give me the strength to push forward in my time of weakness. Because I am not a man who just gives up on love. Who just gives up on the one I want to share eternity with especially when it comes to a woman like Zaire who I loved before she became a thought of God/Amun Ra. And when she finally became that thought, I labored hard, effortlessly and dedicatively just to take part in her creation.

THE TRIALS & TRIBULATIONS

Zaire put me through so much. I was suffering both mentally and physically. I would go for days without eating. When I finally ate, I still lacked the nutrient value that only the nourishment of her love could give.

I didn't want food: a substance which promotes growth, provides energy, repairs body tissues and maintains life. I wanted love; her love. And I was willing to starve myself to death, through any speculative possibilities if I couldn't be fed the love I so craved and hunger for.

In the processing of not eating, I lost a considerably amount of weight. I went from looking like a mere manifestation of God/Amun Ra, to the shameful brittle look of a domesticated animal. My appearance got so bad, I had to glue my eyes shut because I couldn't bear to look at the image which bore my reflection in the bedroom mirror.

Zaire love had completely taken over me. And by all means, my appearance had shown that.

Mentally, it was the same as what I was going through physically. The only difference, I was losing my mind. I would wander the streets of Montgomery with a picture of her asking people did they see Zaire. I eventually notified the police and had them put out a missing person report. Unexpectedly, three days later I was arrested for filing a false report on a woman I knew wasn't missing...but was really at home.

A week later, Zaire picked me up from jail and asked, "Nubian, why did you file a missing report on me?"

I replied, "Because missing you is more than just missing you, it's a reflection of who I am and what I'm going through."

She dropped me off at my apartment and went home. I prayed that she would call when she got there. But she never did. So I cried myself to sleep hoping to find her in my dreams.

I awakened at 4:00am finding it hard to cry and fall asleep at the same time. I got out of bed and decided to take a long walk to narrate a mental concept of love. Not surprisingly, I found myself at Zaire's front door wondering if she was on the opposite side holding her pillow imaging it was me.

My intention was to knock and ask if I could come in, however, I couldn't build up the courage to do so. I eventually left and walked back to my apartment to get some rest. The rest was to no avail. I stayed awake thinking about Zaire, missing Zaire, wanting Zaire, longing for Zaire, and needing Zaire. When the sun came up, I popped a few sleeping pills because I was physically and mentally drained.

POSSIBILITIES

There are so many possibilities in any given relationship. Some are endless. Some are short live. Sadly, mine was short lived. And like the great poet, Black-Sun once said:

"How you live your life today reflects how you will live your life tomorrow."

Like the love bird I was, I lived my life soaring without stretched wings dedicated fully and completely to Zaire. Hell, I couldn't bear to have it any other way because my love was a possibility in and of itself; such a possibility that I felt my love even encompass the impossible.

And guess what? My stupid azz tried to do the impossible, but it turned out to be a disaster.

If my memory serves me right, it was in the beginning of spring when this disaster occurred. The weather was warm and breezy, a manifestation of the sun's glories impact upon nature.

Zaire was having a picnic in Oak Park with a few of her sorority sisters; at least that's what I thought. Anyway, I thought I would surprise Zaire by parachuting from a small plane that I had rented and land in the mist of her picnic to ask her to marry me.

As the airplane pilot flew over Oak Park, just above Zaire's picnic, I parachuted from the plane and landed on top of a business engagement she was having with a multi-million dollar client who was interested in buying property in the Downtown area.

"You idiot!" Zaire screamed at the top of her lungs after her client called the deal off. "Don't you know you just cost me a hundred grand?"

"I didn't know," I said, dumbfounded. I tried adamantly to explain myself. However, my fraudulent explanation was useless. The hundred grand she lost was the only thing weighing heavily on her mind. I couldn't blame her; it was my fault.

"Yea, you never know." she said walking off.

Later on that evening, I made the choice to pawn the ring I bought that would have consummated our love, or for better words, brought our love to the highest possible point of perfection.

When the ring was sold, I deposited the $100,000.00 into her account. She never thanked me. Some unregretable regret? Perhaps.

Nonetheless, I still believe there exists a possibility where I could find a way to make her forgive me in attaining a conceivable dialogue. So I tried calling her. Even sent wireless e-mails. It took Zaire months before she finally returned my calls.

Our conversations was pictorial...water colored at its best, painted with a blended touch of sweet talk. Just to hear her voice made me feel like a high school student studying psychology and art in the form of committed emotions. It was also the only time I felt whole, but not the only time I would feel incomplete.

INCOMPLETE

My inappropriate present led me to the idea that, although I made up half of our relationship, which created our WHOLE. I still felt incomplete.

I gave so much of myself while Zaire gave so little. Only God/Amun Ra knows how foolish in love I was with this woman. And I had the audacity to think, that being foolishly in love with Zaire would somehow make me whole. Depressingly, it only made me incomplete; whereas, I had evolved through so many evolutions only to witness and struggle with the half of me that became fragmented.

With all that said, I still needed Zaire. I needed her to make that which was "incomplete" complete. It never happened. And I was left to contemplate would I ever be complete at all.

During much contemplation my head begin to ache. I took all kinds of pain relievers. When I realized it was my heart that was really aching, I took pain relievers for chest pains. When that didn't work, I tried depression pills. When the depression pills didn't work, I tried meditation. When the meditation didn't work, I tried acupuncture.

I had tried everything listed above. Yet, none of it could cure me of the feeling of being incomplete. None of it cured me from the incompleteness that would make my life void and vacant. Make my life so insecure.

So primitive.

So worthless.

But most of all, so hazardous.

My life felt like a black-hole disobedient in its quest not to conform to the laws of a universal love that begs to make me complete. How long could I hold on before I begin to fade away and become fully and completely incomplete? Would it be worth it to sacrifice what little that remains of me? I am not immune to being incomplete. So why take the risk?

Maybe because I am still waiting for the second, the minute, the hour, the day, for Zaire to make me whole.

THE GAP

There was a huge gap in the relationship me and Zaire shared. And, as much as I tried to fill that gap, nothing worked. The gap got bigger and bigger.

It was obvious I needed to do something fast. Or lose the one woman whom I valued so much; I couldn't afford that. Not in this recession of loneliness and economic death. I could cope with a broke bank account but not a broken heart.

So, at all cost, I was determined to do whatever it took to sustain our relationship. I had to devise a plane.

I begin to bridge the gap.

What other choice did I have? Zaire was all that I lived for. I wasn't going to let a "gap" isolate me from having the air that I breathe (her breath). Or the liquid breath I drink (her kisses), which came in the form of hydronated love.

When the first plan failed, I immediately followed suit with another one. As opposed to bridging the gap, I decided to shorten it. It took some time, but the second plan worked. Me and Zaire begin to share endless moments of quality time together. We went out to movies. Went to spoken word cafes. Took long vacations to exotic islands. When we weren't doing these things, the two of us stayed at my apartment and cuddled up together and made poetic love until the sun brought its presence upon our morning.

When she used to come from work to my apartment after a long day of property selling, I would massage her back, rub her feet with baby oil and at times, I would even scratch or play in her hair to ease a bit of her mental tension.

I would also cook for her, do the dishes, the laundry and fold the towels, blankets and sheets neatly.

After all the pampering and cleaning, we would make poetic love again. However, instead of penetration I would give her oral sex. I would use my tongue, stroking sweetly on her g-spot. Sometimes for hours until my teeth catch a cavity.

Things were going good for the both of us. But like all good things, they must come to the end.

Mine did and the gap was just the beginning of my problems.

ALL GOOD THINGS MUST COME TO AN END

Does it have to? And to what end? Do all things *must* come to an end? Does this include love? Does this include happiness?

Does this include the time me and Zaire shared? Heart brokenly, yes. Time became a brutal part of my end. It went by in stark durations.

I aged quickly. Grey hair began to articulate my well being and where it would grow.

I was in my twenties so you can imagine how a young man at my age would react to such a phenomena.

I eventually dyed every grey hair I could find that shaped my *external* appearance. Knowing very well I couldn't hide what was going on *internally*. Like suicidal thoughts for instance. I quickly brushed those thoughts aside because the afterlife held too many unwanted answers. Besides, my love in living for Zaire was greater than my love for dying for Zaire. Anyway, one should never end their life for the one they love but rather, end their life WITH the one they love.

But what other choice did I have. Life can seem so worthless without the one you love. You don't come in a relationship to dedicate part of your life with a person. You come in a relationship to dedicate your whole life with that person. Now, and even until the end.

But my life was coming to an end, emotionally that is. It hurt so bad not to have Zaire. The hurt was like a withering flower where water and light from the sun are unconscious of its existence.

I could deal with loving Zaire. But not losing her. I couldn't accept that as a part of my reality. I couldn't except that all good things must come to an end.

Why can't it be, that all BAD things must come to an end? I guess that is the way nature intended it to be. I guess I have to be less carelessly in love. And maybe then, just then! All the good things Zaire and I shared want come to an end.

Who knows, maybe the ending will be never-ending.

Whether all good things come to an end or not. I learned one thing:

Love doesn't come with a warranty.

FIVE WISHES

On a Sunday night I sat in my apartment to celebrate my 21st birthday alone. Zaire came by only to leave a gift at the front door. I guess she wasn't interested in celebrating my birthday with me.

I sat the gift on top of the kitchen table and then open it. Inside was a cake with five candles and the words *HAPPY BIRTHDAY* inscribed in childish colors. I took the five candles to be symbolic. So I lit each candle carefully, in order to blow one out at a time.

I took a deep breath and blew out my first wish: I wish there were no more trials and tribulations.

I took a deep breath and blew out my second wish: I wish there were more possibilities.

I took a deep breath and blew out my third wish: I wish there were no times when I felt incomplete.

I took a deep breath and blew out my fourth wish: I wish there were no gap.

I took a deep breath and blew out my fifth wish: I wish there are no truths in all good things must come to an end.

I was confused whether these wishes would come true or not. I felt after the third wish Zaire had taken me to a decaying state anyway. And that, any trials and tribulations without possibilities or love would not make only a man incomplete, but God as well.

Though love may seem courteous, it means more when you're loving somebody and somebody is loving you back in return.

By the time I had blown out the fourth and fifth wish. I sensed Zaire's love for me had gone sour and no amount of love I give would get me any love in return. But I should have paid more attention to the warning signs. Life teaches us that any gap in a relationship ensures that all good things must come to an end.

ZAIRE'S DIARY

Zaire came by my apartment with her pissy and respiratory attitude talking shit. Saying she wanted her diary back.

I told her I wasn't giving her a got-damn thang until she phoned Rena Davenport, a beautiful, 40 year old psychologist who helped men in broken relationships get over the one they love.

Zaire thought, or assumed, I was sleeping with Ms. Davenport and got highly jealous. Zaire's jealousy led her to say all kind of harsh and nasty words to Ms. Davenport. When she wouldn't phone Ms. Davenport to apologize, I took her diary.

"Open this door, you black bastard!" Zaire screamed. "I know you're in there. Claiming your azz love me but you're laying up with some old azz woman who gonna give you worms."

I sat still not answering.

She tried to use the key I gave her but I had changed the locks months ago as Ms. Davenport suggested. "Go away, Zaire." I said pressing my lips to the door.

"Not until you give me my got-damn diary."

"Are you going to apologize to Rena Davenport?"

"Can a penis not get hard?" Zaire answered.

"Well in that case," I said, "You're not, getting your diary back."

"Fuck you, azz-hole." Zaire said storming from the door.

I left from the door, sat back down and picked up Zaire's diary. I know when women write things in their personal journals or diaries it is consider sacred. But so was our love sacred and Zaire didn't seem to care about that. I need to vent a little anyhow. So this is a perfect way to get some get back.

I open her diary to the middle of the book. Her hand writing was elegant. The color of the pen she used was purple-passion. I felt a little guilty about reading her diary. The guilt soon faded the moment I read these words in her diary:

How can I let him tempt me
Blinded by microscopic intimacy
Although I knew the answer
I was persuaded to listen to my desires
His touch was so warm
Has each page somehow became a y-chromosome
Masculine in its natural form
In each page of my dairy he ensures me it has
For he's culturally painting pictures of my present, future and past
Stating I been mis-educated
And need to be de-educated
Before I can be re-educated
I thought were we somehow intellectually related
I wrote further to see
Because killing him is killing me
He said he would abbreviate my soul
Into my mind where only he control
Mentally I thirst and unfold
To drink words that pours from his lips
Draped in the color of his skin, laced with hieroglyphs
I sip
Then took
The thoughts I wrote in my dairy book
Yet my beauty and love create consciousness in physical words
Which I use to promote a love he tries hard to deserve
But behind my beauty and love lies the secret to my name
That comforts him in his time of pain.

I closed her diary to ponder on what I read. Quite naturally she was writing about me. Those words she wrote spoke volumes. Those words also told me she knew I was foolishly in love with her and would narrowly do anything to keep her.

I never knew she was into poetry, let alone that she writes words in an architecture, shelter inventive way. I write poetry too. Mainly Spoken Word, contaminated over associated jazz. I think a poet can better connect more spiritually and mentally with their audience when music is introduced in the background.

I have no music to leave in her diary. But I will write some Spoken Word in her diary as a response to her ego-tripping azz poetry that she wrote about me.

I turned to an empty page in her diary and wrote the title of my Spoken Word called:

"GANGSTA LOVE"

She told me to pour consciousness into her river
As if I was drinking from the Nile
Although her smile
Is so bright it could melt the sun
She whispered, "gangsta love mix with revolution has just begun
And want be televised."
Heartbreakers are being crucified
By GDs, vice lords, bloods and Crips
Driving through with platinum chains and satin whips:
Some press cruise control
To unload
Glock-40s with gangsta love bullet holes
But while they role on 20s
I role up conscious blunts to keep my mind spinning
That's why on cloud nine, with the nine is where you'll find me
A team of broken hearts, cut-throats and killahs behind me
Diamond up, spiritually dressed up, bullet proof vest up
Throw your set up

Ervin Nubian Holloway

Mines is the gangsta love black power fist
Black power, gangsta love monogamist
Longing for the love I miss.

THE KEY TO HOLDING ON BY LETTING GO

It may seem easy. But not for a man who has allergies in being without Zaire. Watery eyes and running nose are my most frequent symptoms. Similar to the emotional collapse of a hospitalized victim who has been favorably manipulated by pollinated love, symbolic of the *flower* I have tattooed just beneath my crushing six-pack (abs).

I got this flower tattooed for two reasons. (1) I read where a poet beautifully illustrated to a woman: My love is like a flower it grows. And (2) I seen how a flower never lets go of the *soil* it belongs to. It withers and dies, constantly holding on to which it came.

A few of my friends told me the tatted flower was too feminine for my harmonic masculinity. I told them so was love. It is made up of words such as affection, fondness, fidelity, emotion, sentiment, tenderness, gentle, sweet, nurturing, compassionate, and sensitive; all are the qualities/traits a woman used as a "means" of communication in expressing her love toward her mate. But my friends replied, "But a man loves for different reasons." I turned my back towards them, paused for a moment and said, "No, a man loves for the same reasons." Then walked off, got in my car and drove to visit Rena Davenport.

Rena Davenport's office was redecorated from when I first seen it. She wore a sleek fitted dress suit, black in color; that made her feminine body the object of beauty.

She told me to have a seat.

I sat down. The plush, cushion sofa was soft as usual.

"How are you today, Nubian?" She asked.

I looked at her jet black skin, the color of the night sky when a falling star races across the heavens and said, "Fine, I guess."

"Mmmm, I see. Care to talk about it?"

"I wouldn't know where to start."

"Start first by saying what's on your mind." Rena Davenport replied.

"My mind is chained to my heart and won't let go."

Rena Davenport sighed, "Nubian, being in love is truly a drug. And just like Meth, Cocaine and other narcotics, it can make you feel alert, energetic and powerful; in the constant use and abuse of love, it can cause hyperactivity, paranoia, sleeplessness, agitation, aggressive behavior, manic depression, anxiety and occasionally stress-related symptoms. Both "love" and "drug" can cause your brain cells to release chemicals to make you feel good. Over a period of time, just like drugs, love can impair your inability to feel pleasure without love. This often results in loneliness or the key to holding on by letting go.""

"Sounds like I need rehab as opposed to psychological assessment. Are there any 'Love Rehabs' floating around in this country." I said, rather jokingly.

"I am being serious here, Nubian. Love is a strong drug that deals with the central nervous system, causing a speedy, painstakingly, excessive feeling of either well-being and happiness or worthlessness and joylessness. At times you may feel self-assured, arrogant. This is when the insecure feelings about yourself quickly vanish. Yet, the feelings created by your self-assurance and arrogance easily dissolve into a grievous pain. More than a million people die each year behind love related symptoms such as: high-blood pressure, nervous brake-downs, loneliness, severe headaches, chest pains, shortness of breath, suicides and abusive relationships."

I held my head down pondering on the things that Rena Davenport spoke to me. Her words hit me hard, penetrating the shield that protected the addictive, physical and mental aspect of my emotions. Rena Davenport was right. And the only thing I could say to her was "I never looked at love as being a drug."

"We seldom do, Nubian. But, my question to you is, do you wanna get off this drug?"

"I can't. I love her too much." I said, raising from the plush cushioned sofa and heading toward the door to leave.

"Wait." Rena Davenport yelled before I closed the door behind me.

I stood half way in the door and said, "Yes."

"I have seen a woman bring a man to the top. But I've also seen a woman bring a man to the bottom."

I slammed the door. I didn't wanna hear no more of what the bio-bitch had to say. I am already at the bottom with or without Zaire. So being addictive to her love is right up my alley. Whether I snort her love, shoot her love, drink her love, or smoke her love, as long as I O/D on her love. I really don't give a shit.

Anyway, the level of distance in a relationship is based not on how addictive you are to the one you love, but how far you're willing to travel in search of love…to hold on to love….or to maintain love.

It is the love in your life that makes you happy. That makes you sad. That makes you cry. That makes you want more. That makes you want less sometimes. That makes you grow. That makes you decay. That makes you feel like dying. That makes you feel like living. That makes you Conscious. That makes you unconscious. That makes you incomplete. That makes you whole. That makes you feel young. That makes you feel old. That makes you feel strong. That makes you feel weak. That makes you feel absence. That makes you feel present. That makes you feel protected. That makes you feel afraid. But most of all that makes you feel love even though there's a key to holding on by letting go.

But, no one said love would be easy. There will be some ups & downs even in the best of relationships.

So the hell with Rena Davenport. I'll do this shit on my own. Paying her azz a hundred dollars an hour was too damn much anyway. I can get more from my own individual and personal experience with love.

I'm no dummy. I been in this relationship to long to know that the key to holding on to love can only be achieve by letting go, notwithstanding the fact, that it takes more than love to hold love together.

IT TAKES MORE THAN LOVE TO HOLD LOVE TOGETHER

There's no statement truer than this: It's the little things in a loving relationship that makes you happy, or that you remember and love the most.

I remember so many little things about Zaire. Like the smell of her hair. The way she paints her lips. The way she walks. The sound of her voice. The way she smiles and shrouds me in happiness. The warmth she brings. The clothes she wears. The air she breathes inside of me when am breathless.

Depressingly, theses little things were not enough to hold our love together. Zaire had drifted away and my world became a complete mess.

I became anti-social. I begin to live in my own isolated world where no sun would shine. No moon would glow. No stars would guide me. No oceans I could sail on. No rivers I could cross to. No shores I could reach in case I started drowning. No clock to turn back the hands of time. No moments to share. And no calendar to mark the day I cried in order to hold what I knew was worth holding together.

But, isn't love enough to hold or even sustain a relationship together? What more can a man offer a woman if it isn't love? Physical things will fade (money-cars-clothes). Mental things will be forgotten (questions-answers-reason whys). But love is spiritual, that immortal aspect that ensures your right to live among the God[s] where love never fades and want be forgotten.

I doubt the God[s] would want me to live among them considering the condition I am in. And considering how heaven would be once am gone, (destructive and dying).

And I know you're probably saying why didn't I listen to Rena Davenport. Believe me I know I should have. The opportunity was there. Subconsciously, I don't think I went to Rena Davenport's office seeking a way out of love. I went seeking away to hold me and Zaire's love together.

I was so fucked up over Zaire I would have listen to any one. Hell, if someone said to me, "Hey Nubian, try tape it would hold your love together."

I would have tried it.

If someone said to me, "Look Nubian, I am telling you. If you try crazy-glue it would hold your love together."

I would have tried that to.

If someone said to me, "Don't tell nobody I told you this, Nubian. But if you use tire-glue and let the girl who you're in love with run over your azz. I know for sure it will either hold your love together or kill your stupid azz.*"

I would have hesitated leisurely for a moment and did that to. I would worry about the results later.

"People" do some wild and crazy shit to hold love together. And, I'm no exception to the rule. The only thing is, I don't play by the rules. Because rules were made to be broken, but love on the other hand is not. For it is a bond that binds halves of a broken heart together. And no one more desperately than me needed his heart that has been shattered into a thousand pieces, to be bond, bind and held together.

I wrote some Spoken Word (poetry) below to convey to the reader as to how I was feeling.

I'm crying
Even though I don't have no eyes to
Am dying
How do you expect me to live without you
Battling with my own uncertainty
There's no love growing where this heart use to be
Don't you know love is best serve

When it blossom for the whole world to see
So come and share the Garden of Eden with me
And I will give you paradise for all eternity

Incarcerated heart
Although we're so close
It feels like we're worlds apart
Armageddon, my world has now come to an end
No life, no air, no oxygen
How can I ever breathe without you
All I can ever do is think about you
So come and share the Garden of Eden with me
And I will give you paradise for all eternity

Should I move on?

But…

Which way do I turn, right, left? Do I go East, South, North or West?

It matters little. They say men are incapable of settling down anyway. Having a committed relationship is to apologetic for them in such a global, dominated women society. So moving on for them becomes unsparing and ultraconservative.

<u>Conservative</u>

adj. 1. tending to resist Or oppose change.

Not me. I wasn't going nowhere not as long as Zaire remains in Montgomery, Alabama. And I am certainly not opposed to change. I knew things change. Life change. Thoughts change. Attitudes change. People change. The world as we know it is changing right before our very eyes.

But guess what?

Love never changes. And I refuse to move on in spite of my many difficulties with Zaire. I love her to much, and no force on God's green earth will move me. I have sacrifice to much already. Adversity and deep-seated victimization has been a constant struggle for me during the mid-election of our relationship. So why give up now! There's just too much at stake. I can't go nowhere; I am officially grounded. Not even god can move me.

Because my intentions are not to be move under no circumstances, rather it is spiritual or physical. So if I have sinned or transgressed by saying this, I repent not in the favor of being forgiving, but rather in the favor of being love.

And that love can only come from Zaire. A love I regard as my fortress, as my shield, as my sanctuary, as my heaven, and as my protection when I have transgressed against god.

Maybe, I'll go far as to transgress and get on my knees and pray to Zaire. Or in the alternative, tattoo her dreams in biblical scriptures across my shoulders; anything not to move on. Anything to stay put and live my life knowing there is nothing on earth or in heaven that could offer a realistic approach under such spiritual extremities my moving on without Zaire would cause.

Therefore, let me be baptized in Zaire name. Let me be anointed in the joyful tears she often cried when I made her happy. And likewise, bless by the words that populate this physical body when her spirit becomes my Genesis. And her soul becomes my Revelation.

MY GENESIS - MY REVELATION

Zaire is my Alpha and my Omega. She's my beginning and my ending. To tell the truth, I never loved a woman in such a spiritual way.

It got so bad, (this loving her in a spiritual way), I said to myself, "if I could biblically read her it would be Proverbs Chapter 3 verse 15-16-17 & 18."

I didn't stop there. I decided to create a whole religion faith surrounding her. It would not be Christian or Islam. It would be Zairism, mixed with a brush of the two faiths above as if I was an artist painting her beauty across the heavens.

I told myself I would convert those who were interest in this new found faith of Zairism, that Zaire is their Creatress and she has breathe the breath of life in all humans. That she had created the world in five days base on the five senses. And on the six and seven day she rested so she could spend time with me. Also, I went as far as to creating a religious symbol. The Christians have the cross. The Muslims have the crescent moon and star. Why shouldn't I have a symbol representing Zairism? With hours of drawing and sketching, I finally came up with the perfect symbol.

Next I had to write, or formulate, a Holy Book like the Christians did with the Bible and the Muslims did with the Qu'ran. It took months to construct the Holy Book. It would have taken longer had I not decided to use Zaire's dairy instead. And use the one I wrote: "A GUIDE TO WORSHIPPING THE BLACK WOMAN" as a follow up or a manual to Zaire's dairy.

The purpose of the manual would consist of these:

1. Day of worship would not be Sunday, but November 10th.
2. Rituals.
3. Incense burning.
4. Fasting.
5. Taking time out for the poor, sick, and old.

6. Meditation.

I felt that the (6) listed above would be best suited for those who are willing to join Zairism.

With that part of the new religion faith taken care of, I had to comprise laws that will govern all practitioners & believers. I then constructed two mahogany wooden tablets of reddish-brown color similar to what biblical scholars "claim" God gave to Moses on the Mount Sinai: Exodus19.

Art by D. L. Ahamma

Then came the 'quest,' or as the Christians would: say, "spreading the gospel." I went from door to door like a Jehovah's Witness does when they are preaching that the kingdom of God is at hand. But, every door I went to I was turned down or had the door slammed in my face.

A few people listened. A punk who tried to illicit my phone and email address. A cracker who eventually spit on me. And an old black woman who said, "Chile, that's my granddaughter you tryin'na get me to worship. She ain't stun yo ass. Now, run alone before I call the police on ya."

The next day Zaire called me going off over the phone asking, "Nubian, why the hell you go over my grand-mother's house crying in front of her because I haven't been spending time with you?"

"Wait a minute. Where did you get some shit like that from?"

"My grandmother, nigga! Don't be going over my grandmother's house worrying her about our crumbling relationship. She has enough problems as it is."

"Your grandmother is lying her azz off. I didn't..."

"Don't you dare call my grandmother a liar." Zaire said, cutting me off. "She's a devout Christian. She has no reason to lie on your tired azz."

"Well, she did." I snapped.

"Well, my azz. Bye, nigga. I was going to let you come over. But since you did some shit like that. Fuck, you."

<<<CLICK>>>

Like a fool. I called her ill-behaving azz back. But she either hung up in my face or let the phone ring.

They say blood is thicker than water. There was no way I could compete with her grandmother. But why did her grandmother instigate a lie like

I
Thou shall daily pay homage to Zaire

II
Thou shall love Zaire with all thou mind, body & soul

III
Thou shall have no creatress besides Zaire

IV
Thou shall remember the Sabbath November 10th
and keep it holy.

V
Thou shall have a relastingship
opposed to a relationship

VI
Thou shall always remain faithful to Zaire

VII
Thou shall keep thou heart pure so Zaire may dwell therein

VIII
Thou shall honor Zaire so thou days may be longer

IX
Thou shall through selfless sacrifice give back to Zaire

X
Thou shall keep thou self holy
because Zaire is holy

that? The day I came by her house with the religious intention to convert her to Zairism is the first time I ever seen her.

But she knew exactly who I was. How?

I call Zaire back to find out. She answered the phone on the first ring. "Hello." Zaire said.

"Bout time you answer the phone."

"I got tired of your azz calling. Now, what the hell do you want?"

The tone of her voice made me sick to my stomach causing me to have one of those nauseating moments. But I swallowed hard and said, "How did your grandmother know it was me that day?"

"From all the pictures we took, stupid. Plus I told her everything about you. More bad than good."

"Bad!" I exclaimed. "What bad things have I done?"

"Calling me all the damn time, not giving me room to breathe, sending roses to my house five days a week; you name it."

"I do these things because I love you. And if loving you is bad, tell me what should I do to make it good?"

"Sell your soul to the devil." Zaire replied.

"Why should I when you're the one causing me hell." I said, hanging up and destroying all the religious ideas and concepts I had created of her. Realizing, I had created myself in the image and likeness that she wanted me to be as oppose to the image and likeness that I wanted her to be. Somehow, this led to my insanity.

Ervin Nubian Holloway

MY INSANITY

What can make you more less or derange than love? Wherefore, you try to piece together the most prophetic feeling of not being saneless, mindless, senseless, in order to anticipate the best possible outcome. The million dollar answer - INSANITY ITSELF.

Insanity

noun. 1. grave disorder of the mind that impairs one's capacity to function safely or normal in any emancipated society.

I guess you could say that the word above is non-hypocritical of what I've become, a lunatic for a woman who I'm soo crazy in love with. Love leaves me no room for being sane anyway. Even if it did, loving Zaire would eventually make me psychotic and delusional for she has psychologically became a mental part of me.

Although, I know it's insane to give up my sanity for Zaire, It becomes apocalyptic for me and trance like once I'm held hostage by her hypnotic love and my depleting emancipation.

Maybe I could emerge from some form of exodus that could very well eliminate my insanity for Zaire. Sadly however, the word (exodus) is too of broad expression. For where would my insanity lead or have me migrate to?

I could blindly follow my heart. But my insanity would only punctuate a mental image of Zaire where-ever I go. Considering the fact there's no forfeiture that my insanity can incur at the inexpense of loving a woman like Zaire.

You see, I'd rather be mentally insane *with a touch* of Zaire's love than to be mentally sane *without a touch* of her love. Because Zaire is my sanity and my sanity is the result of my insanity to be resurrected.

ABBREVIATE MY SOUL

Bring me your smile as a symbol of the sun when I grow cold
Melt away my pain
Because life without you is driving me insane
And I don't have the capacity
To try to use my pain
To defy the law of gravity

My insanity

A degree of mental malfunctioning to most
Maybe a sign of losing hope
And to some
It maybe loneliness infused with storms
That are held hostage by drowning skies
In which thoughts of you never dies
And consciousness is infused with rain
That leaks from my eyes
Causing a climate that want change

My insanity

RESURRECTION

Months have passed without Zaire. For me it feels like time has rehabilitated itself to stand still.

My love for her still persist though, whether there's an hourglass or a clock on the wall. For time doesn't determine when love will end. Love can be resurrected at any second, minute or hour.

Resurrect vb. 1 to restore to life <he held true to the belief that his heart would be literally resurrected.>

Consequently, time is not on my side. And the resurrection of my heart is in suspended animation. I too now stand still.

The belief in the afterlife is my belief in love. All feelings and affections are scarred. I am a registration to my own inadequate emotions to effectively heal or resurrect itself. I have become only the body. A shell. A empty vessel. A carcass. Ejaculated flesh. Stiff remains. And an immaterial substance *where the immaterial becomes immaterial (Matrix exerpt).*

All the above, (what I've become) is the cause and effect of the undue and untowering results of this empty vessel (body of water) and this shell (body of love). To resuscitate and resurrect itself from a heart that refuses to let go when letting go is so hard to do. Nothing can resurrect me from this emotional death anyway. I will need something to hold on to. There's no rope that the heart has when you feel like you're dying or losing your grip without the one you love.

Resurrection then becomes useless. No dying heart can never truly be raise. Not if the voice it is emotional attach refuse to (call) it from a loving resting place. To paraphrase what I am saying, I'm calling out for Zaire to bring me back to life. She is the only one that can resurrect me; the only one that can resuscitate me; the only one that can make me immortal; and, the only one, when all else has failed, that can articulate a living interpretation as to the meaning of my *existence*.

THE MEANING OF MY EXISTENCE

A very special niece of mine, Nikki, gave me a few tickets to attend a two-day seminar. I honestly didn't want to go. But my niece is my heart, so I had no other choice but to attend.

I got dressed in a tailor-made suit, threw on my gators and headed out the door. It took me a little over twenty minutes to get there. I got out my car, put some coins in the meter, looked myself over and gracefully walked inside the Civic Center.

The place was jammed pack. I took the first seat I saw. A lady I sat next to said, "You're going to enjoy this."

I smiled weakly, "I hope so." I then closed my eyes in hope of sleeping through the whole seminar.

But that wasn't about to happen. Not if it depended on the lady I was sitting next to. "Wake up." The lady said, shaking me. "There she is. The seminar about to start."

"There who is?" I asked, in a drowsy state, not knowing who the hell she was referring to.

"Joy Stone." she pointed toward the stage.

I looked up. And was behold by a *sleeping* beauty.

Sleep n. 1 the natural periodic suspension of consciousness during which the powers of the body are restored.

I had to constantly rub my eyes to be sure I wasn't dreaming or still drowsy. This falling angelic beauty was a curse to a heaven filled with immortal gods but a blessing to an earth fill with immortal men. Oh how I wanted her to cover me with her wings that we both might fly away and take our rightful place as rulers of the heavens.

Miraculously, this was the only time Zaire didn't cross my mind.

"OK," she spoke. "How are you ladies and gentlemen doing out there tonight?"

"Fine." The crowd roared.

"Good." she smiled. "I am Joy Stone, public speaker and seminar expert. I will get right to my topic, 'Existence.' I want you all to listen attentively." Joy Stone paused for a minute then continued. "We all base our existence on a host of reasons. Some base their existence on the fear that there's no life after death. Some base their existence on the fact that this is the only existence they know. Others base their existence on faith, dreams, wealth, love. On family, friends, wife, husband, etc. Now what do you base your existence on? Anybody care to elaborate?"

The Civic Center grew silent. Not a sound resonated throughout the whole building. The shuffle of people moving to find comfort in their seat is the only thing that could be heard.

"You." Joy Stone pointed.

I turned in my seat widely, hoping that this angelic creature wasn't referring to me.

"Me." I pointed at myself.

"Yes, you. Don't be shy. Come on up here."

I walked nervously to the stage. She took her hands in mine bringing me within her presence. I could smell the scent of her perfume. It was sweet, feminine and chocolate, the same as the color of her skin. Her hair was sophisticatedly tied in a bun. I was breathless when she asked, "What's your name?"

Gasping, I said, "Nubian."

Noticing my nervousness, Joy Stone whispered in a low tone so that the audience wouldn't hear her, "Don't worry Nubian. It's your first time. Just take a deep breath, exhale. And everything will be ok."

I breathed long and hard, gazed at her beauty and said, "I am fine now."

"Good. Now am going to ask you a question. I want you to say your answer loud enough for the audience to hear. Are you ready?"

"I think so."

"What do you base your existence on, Nubian?" Joy Stone said, gazing deep into my eyes.

I met her gaze. "Zaire."

"And why do you base your existence on Zaire?"

I sighed. "Because I love her."

Joy Stone turned toward the audience. "We will deal with Nubian's second answer first." She then turned back to me, "Nubian, love is an emotion; something that is share between two existence people. And because of love, they will rob the heavens for each other, they will drink the oceans dry for each other, they will steal God's eyes for each other, they will dip words into poetry and bring forth each other names, they will make their dreams come true for each other, they will give to eternity that which love has kept secret for each other, and lastly, but not least, they will exist for each other."

The audience got out their seats and start applauding. One old lady yell out, "You go sister."

After the audience calmed down, Joy Stone said to me, "Nubain, you said you base your existence on Zaire. Can you truly and honestly say to me and the audience that Zaire bases her existence on you?"

I walked off the stage and exited the Civic Center. I didn't want to answer a question that I knew I didn't have an answer for.

The next day Joy Stone came by my apartment. How she got my address was unknown to me and I didn't bother to ask, either. Just seeing her was a good enough reason for me. Because beauty has a compromising way of curing a man's world seen through loneliness.

We talked. Not only that day, but day after day. It became routine for us. There was never a dull moment. The more we talked, the more I got to know her.

She told me how speaking to so many people gave her the most rewarding feeling she'd ever felt. I found her to be so genuine, so caring. She reminded me so much of Zaire when we first met.

But those days I mention to you earlier, turned into months. My world no longer seemed lonely.

We would go shopping. I would pick out the best lash-defining mascara, liner and shadow. She was surprised to know that a man of my statue knew about mascara. I would take her to Tiffany's and buy her matching earrings, rings and necklace studded in black, blue and red diamonds. She did the same and bought me Cartier wrist watch with the bracelet to match.

We did so much together I found myself wanting to spend more and more time with Joy Stone. And I did. And I was beginning to know the meaning of my *existence* and to tell Zaire that *it can't be all of you and none of me*.

IT CAN'T BE ALL OF YOU & NONE OF ME

Zaire came by while I was baking a cake for Joy's birthday. I let her in. At any other time I would have been happy to see her. But, not this time. I was focus on Joy and all that I had planned for her birthday.

I took the cake out the oven. "Smells good." Zaire said. "Who is it for?"

"I don't think that's any of your business, Zaire." I said, placing the cake on the table. "So tell me, why are you here?"

"I haven't seen you in awhile. You haven't called. I was worry about you."

"Now you're worry about me. Don't you think it's a little bit too late for that from what you put me through?"

Zaire came close to me. Close enough where she could touch my face. "I'm sorry. I thought long and hard about it, realizing I was wrong. You're too good of man for me to be losing."

I moved her hand away from my face, walked past her, reached in the cabinet to put some icing on Joy's birthday cake. "Is that your excuse, Zaire? I'm too good of a man." I said, rather angrily "Well, I must not have been *that* good of a man if it took you *this* long to realize it." I said, angrily again.

"Shit, I said I'm sorry. What else do you want me to say?"

"Goodbye would be a great start." I said, popping the top to spread the icing on Joy's cake.

"You can't be serious?" Zaire responded unbelievingly.

"As a heart attack," I replied.

"Don't do this to me, Nubian please. I know you still love me, you have to. I admitted I was wrong. We can work this out, can't we?"

"I tried, Zaire. Lord knows I tried. But you wanted things your way. You took my love for granted. It was Zaire's way or no way," I walked out the kitchen toward the front door and opened it.

She followed minutes later.

"Now it's my way." I said directing her to leave.

"Nubian, don't," Zaire cried out, throwing her arms around my neck.

I tried pulling her arms away but she held on tight. "Let go, Zaire." I said, struggling to pull her arms lose.

"Please baby, I'm sorry." I could feel her tears rolling down my neck. "I'll do anything to make it right."

"You can't right the wrong, Zaire," I blurted out finally braking free of her arms.

She dried her eyes. "But aren't wrongs forgiven?"

I stood silent for a moment. "Some are."

"In that case, could you forgive me for all the wrong I caused and I promise you I will do right this time. I promise Nubian, with all my heart, and all my soul."

"You see, Zaire, that's your problem. It's always Zaire- Zaire- Zaire and never Nubain- Nubain- Nubian. Well, not any more. I will no longer let you consume or devour my life, or my love, period!"

"You're saying that it's over, Nubian?"

"No. I'm saying that it can't be all of you and none of me. And that loving you.....isn't worth losing me. Bye, Zaire," I said, closing the ending chapter to my life. And opening the beginning chapter in my life.

Ervin Nubian Holloway

CONCLUSION

1. If you're willing to (get) love
2. Make sure you're willing to (give) love.
3. And if you're willing to (give) love
4. Make sure you (get) the love you deserve.

Ervin Nubian Holloway

POETRY a Collection of Poems I wrote to Zaire That She Returned

PRAYER

I prayed a thousand times

But heaven wouldn't listen to these prayers of mines

So I cried

Hoping to drown heaven with my tears.

ACID RAIN

Acid rain

Constantly writing words on my window pane

Telling stories to my tears and your name

Where chapters are waiting to bathe

In an ocean that drips from my page

At a time when my pen tried to save

Books that dream of yesterday.

A SOUND

There's a sound that creates dreams

That over flows

That is like water when it falls

That I run to when it calls

It is able to calm storms

Plant words that will grow in to poems

It is soft and polite

This sound is like magic

Reappearing often in my life

Sometimes floating like a gentle spirit

Reminding me of shared moments when I hear it

It makes those things which are harmful harmless

Giving me a sense of renewed warmness

It is a sound that cools my anger when I'm mad

It fills me with happiness when I'm sad

And when I'm afraid

It tells me there's nothing to fear

It is the sound of your voice

That I hear.

LOST WITHOUT YOU

Pass me a sheet of paper that is unbless

And I'll write to you

How empty is my emptiness

How I'm left to wander throughout the earth

To find the nature of my self-worth

That I once knew

When I became

Lost without you.

I'D RATHER DIE

Death begs not to know my name

As I walk through the after-life and the everlasting pain

Have I became soulless and unwanted by heaven

Or has love just been prolonged

Enabling me to carry on

I rather die today

Than to spend another moment away

I'm so torn

Why was I created?

Why was I born?

In a world without you

Maybe the devil knew…

The hell I would be going through

For I can feel the fire

The burning desire

To pave hell with your heart and laughter

In the search for love and the here-after

Ervin Nubian Holloway

I WILL CRY

I don't know who I am any more

What is life worth living for?

I tried my best to hold on, but nothing seem to work

Nothing seem to stop the pain

Nothing seem to stop the hurt

So I will cry

Until my tears flood the earth

I will cry

Until the day we are one again

But mainly I will cry

Until heaven and earth ends

The clouds I stole from the heaven skies

Have caught the clouds that have formed in my eyes

Have they mistaken my tears for clouds or rain?

Over looking my trials and pain

But how could this be

When there's a climate

Loving You and Loosing Me!

Brewing inside of me

I will cry

Until the day we are one again

But mainly I will cry

Until heaven and earth end

Ervin Nubian Holloway

PREPARED MORNING

Wake up to the sound of laughter

Heard from the voice of an angel

Prepared by the freshness of morning

That became the object

That plants the sun in your mind

Giving me the ability to see

Through the darkness

And my troubling times

Prepared morning asking to be born

To give birth to love

The minute the sun begin to rise

Night no longer knows

How morning is prepared

Night passes

And the morning is awaken by brightness

Excuse me,

I meant to say your smile and likeness

Loving You and Loosing Me!

And your smile is so bright and true

That it could cause the sun to dislike you

But heated dislike can always be undone

For you have a smile that could melt the sun

Prepared morning asking to be born

To give birth to love

The minute the sun begin to rise

Night no longer knows

How morning is prepared

Ervin Nubian Holloway

PAINT BRUSH

Dying to bring you wet music

To prevent this rhythm from melting stars

Behind caged tears and parallel bars

Due to random thermal fears

Gradually forming into molecules of love by abstract ideas.

A paint brush

Flowing outside of time

Glass and paint

Poured over closed eyes and verbs

Not enough time to see what will occur

Through the origin of sexual transmitted words

Often caused by the change in temperature & degree

In order to give you a color of warmness

That has been painted inside of me

A paint brush

Flowing outside of time

I WILL FOLLOW YOU

I will follow you where distance breathes

Bathe you in my words

And be your seed

Grow out of darkness

While your smile gives me light

Be your sun through the day

And your moon through the night

Ask your eyes

Are visions made out of poems?

Make you think my hands are oceans

So I can drown you in my arms.

Ervin Nubian Holloway

OPEN MIND IT

When I write about you

People can't relate to what I have written

They say my poetry is sinfully forbidden

Then they have the nerve to say

In a biblical way

That my poetry need to be stone

I say they are religiously wrong

Be open mind-it

And you won't feel left behind-it

Seek what my poetry dreams

Don't have a understanding

But an overstanding of what they mean

When I bathe

I often bathe in your poetry

Letting words drip from my pen slowly

That they may soothe you

Then move you

Loving You and Loosing Me!

Geographically

In such a capacity

That your ability to absorbed or receive

Would be impossible for you to believe

Be open mind-it

And you won't feel left behind-it

Seek what me poetry dreams

Don't have an understanding

But an overstanding of what they mean

I LOVED YOU BEFORE YOU WERE BORN

Silently I speak

Walking through the night

Calling out your name when I sleep

To say:

"I loved you before you were born"

Before time began

And I will continue to love you

Until time never end

I WILL (*REMIX*)

I will rob the heavens and the sky for you

I will drink the ocean dry for you

I will stop breathing for you

I will walk through fire for you

I will steal god's eyes for you

I will even kill for you

I will dip my words into poetry for you and bring forth your name

I will take away all your hurt and pain

I will place the sun in the palm of my hand and make it beg of you

I will cut both of my arms-and still be able to hold you

I will follow the tears to your eyes so I may know how to comfort you

I will give to eternity that which life has kept secret from you

I will do all I have to do

I'll even turn my back on god for you

I ONLY EXIST BECAUSE OF YOU

The innocence that grows in your eyes

Like a flower when the sun rise

Can only be a story

A book I read once

About your beauty and glory

Written on the pages of heaven

Painted on the canvass of nature

For summer to hold out its arms to spring

To make nature sing

Of soft promises

And a drop of essence

Soaked in warm water

Bathe in your blessing

A glimpse of Mother Nature

A pause for Father Time

To let winter hold out its arms to fall

My whole life through

I only exist because of you

AFRAID TO CRY

Being tough start to apply

When a man like me is afraid to cry

I then becomes alter emotions

Converted into plastic rain

Leaving misty drops

Upon my window-pane

In a way that expresses my longing to give to you

This life that I live through you.

SCENTED WORDS

Scented words

My eyes are crowded with verbs

Where the actions of flowers are able to grow from words

And years wish to be born

And love hid the sun

And time sleep

And hours are turn into days and days into weeks

And for nine months poems rain forth from clouds

And poetry give birth to a child

And syllables are unable to smile

And the earth breathe its last breath

And in the beginning was the word and the word was made flesh

And a young girl has unfilter sex

And now her pregnancy is shown

And he leaves her to raise the child on her own

And now life for her seem to be a chapter in her isolated page

It's either that

Slash, minimal rage

Loving You and Loosing Me!

Or struggle with a father who don't give a fuck

Where she gets her next buck

From unemployment lines or welfare

But "me" I care

Because I write scented words

And I am a poet

Whose eyes are crowded with verbs.

Ervin Nubian Holloway

PAGES

Why do words swim in your eyes?

Drowning this pen that I write with

And who flooded you with dying pages

At a moment when I'm lifeless

NOTHING IS WORTH MORE THAN YOU

To hear your laughter

Would be worth all the happiness shared with God

And a million Christians couldn't convert my loving heart

For some have tried

But all have fail

Not knowing that life without you

Would be a living hell

Nothing is worth more than you

Not even God himself

For the first moment I manifest here on this earth

I knew I would put god second and you first

To most people this might be sinful to say

But in my heart

I think God would want it no other way

Nothing is worth more than you

Not even God himself

When I say that you are worth more than God

I know a lot of people want agree

They would say "don't be so foolish"

But I would happily say

I think God would want it no other way

CHOICE

Where did you come from?

Give me a clue

If I had the choice

To pick heaven or you

It wouldn't take me a second

To pick between the two

POETRY H$_2$O

When liquid words burn slowly

And leave ashes behind

Let me drown you in my poetry

Let me drown you in my mind

Just for a moment

Until I'm able to drown time

Poetry H^{2}O

Written in sacred letters

Symbolizing the flow

Of thoughts and suspended matter

When clouds and poems start their formation

Let me give to you

Word to word resuscitation

That you may have immortality

In a biblical way known by me

Through the breath of life

Loving You and Loosing Me!

Written in my poetry

Poetry H^2O

Written in sacred letters

Symbolizing the flow

Of thoughts and suspended matter

When poetry use subliminal suggestions

I'll mirror you away from superstitious guessing

Into a belief in seven years of poetry

And spiritual reflection

That will enable you to decipher the flow

Of poetry H^2O

TAROT CARDS

Sleep walking through one hundredth (10^{-2}) of a yard

Hearing the shuffle of tarot cards

Falling from my bed

Vices-virtues and elemental forces

Of you in my head

With these aluminum eyes

It's hard for me to describe

The temperature at which tears boil

In a state of emotional turmoil

Prematurely as to what I'm going through

In this life without you

Sleep walking through one hundredth (10^{-2}) of a yard

Hearing the shuffle of tarot cards

Falling from my bed

Depicting vices-virtues and elemental forces

Of you in my head

Loving You and Loosing Me!

I haven't slept in days

Sometimes love can't be awaken from its stubborn ways

Sleeping for me isn't as easy as it seem

Having a dream within a dream

Maybe I'm just sleep walking until you make heaven unfold

Into the awakening of my soul

AM HERE

Until forever stop breathing...

Am here

Even when the sky turn from dawn to evening...

Am here

Until death do us part...

Am here

Through the brake-ups and broken hearts...

Am here

Through the sunny days and bad weather...

Am here

Even when we're not together...

Am here

If you turn your back on me...

Am here

For all eternity...

Am here

Though your joy and pain...

Am here

Loving You and Loosing Me!

When there's no one to blame...

Am here

If you forsake me...

Am here

Even if you hate me...

Am here

When you want things to be ok...

Am here

Especially when things are not going your way...

Am here

When bad things about you pours from somebody's mouth...

Am here

If you wanna get some straightening and knock their asses out...

Am here

No matter what the situation maybe

Or what outcome may appear

I just want you to know...

Am here

SIN

Cover my broken heart from sin

And make me whole again

Tears drop from the sun

Revelation 2001

Prophesying these troubling times for me

As to why these last days of mine are so empty

For time has now exceeded the day's end

Through horoscopes that breast feed sin

Dividing me into 12 days

12-months

And 12 zodiac formations

Bearing the name of the constellation

Which is 30° degrees wide

That will lead me to your side

Cover my broken heart from sin

And make me whole again

NO

There's no door to my house

There's no water leaking from these words

There's no heaven to hold these sins

Does heaven have a heaven?

Let me bare this cross for thee

And I'll walk my heart

Up the stairway that lead me

To you and god

There's no door to my house

There's no water leaking from these words

There's no heaven to hold these sins

Foot prints in my eyes

Religious ceremonies maybe disguise

Here in this soul where prayer is made

Constantly where your spirit bathes

Ervin Nubian Holloway

Inside my altar

Sacrifices are offered

Based on a system of equation

As a substitute for sin

And spiritual migration

POETRY

Poetry....

Like a million heavens

Like the setting of the sun

Searching for that special one

Who would blend the sky with a mixture of dreams?

Occasionally stolen

Occasionally seen

Poetry....

The tears of many words

Dying to be comfort

Dying to be heard

So let me be the answer to your questions

And the godly man

Who will grant you your blessing

Forever

For eternity

Because you are my words

My meaning

My poetry

IF YOU DIDN'T EXIST

I hate to imagine it

How life would be if you didn't exist

I know the sun would turn cold

God would die and grow old

The angel would get no rest

The world would be filled with emptiness

The sky would be filled with pain

The clouds would be filled tears and rain

The moon and stars would never gleam

The birds would never sing

The season would never change

Life would remain the same

Time would cry and stand still

There wouldn't be no reason for me to live

My life would be an empty space

Filled with an abandonment in an empty place

Filled with the unforgotten hope of a broken wish

If you didn't exist

BAPTIZE

Long ago I search for something

In my attempt to find you

But it was hard for you to embrace

Poetry running down my face

So if you see me crying syllables

I'm expressing how miserable

I am without you

I need to be baptize

In your gentle eyes

Too many heavens hold secrets about this dimension

Why am I held in temporary suspension?

I had to ask

I had to move

For I had nothing to lose

Because there is no one who could animate

123

Me from my motionless state

So if you see me crying syllables

I'm expressing how miserable

I am without you

I need to be baptize

In your gentle eyes

I can feel myself not breathing

I can feel my heart not beating

And digesting poetry

Has stop me from eating

I'm expressing that I rather see death

By starving myself

So if you see me crying syllables

I'm expressing how miserable

I am without you

TEARS - TWO THOUSAND & TWELVE

No longer

No more

This pain I bore

My eyes are sore

At a moment when time and space became the voice of something real

Yet time nor space could heal

Watery eyes I held for so many years

And I wanna cry

But no one taught me how to swim in tears

Falling apart

Too many closed doors

Not enough keys to unlock this crying heart

No...

Not any more

This pain I bore

My eyes are sore

Cried too much already

Ervin Nubian Holloway

No balance

Life no longer steady

Future is hard to tell

Tears...

Two thousand and twelve

GRAVITY

Cold nights, somehow time has frozen

My blanket seems to be the only thing keeping me warm

My heart beats no more

God knows!

I wish I could make it like before

When our worlds wasn't worlds apart

And love wrote your name across my heart

And we became as one

Like the setting of the sun

In its stages of immaturity

Gravity

Equates to a drop in temperature

My batter and broken pen

No time to heal these torn pages

My paper never meant so much

Dripping ink has proven such

Ervin Nubian Holloway

Now my emotions melt

My feelings erupt

Now I feel the hot chills of love

Gravity

Equates to a drop in temperature

128

THE UNKNOWN

Pour sand into my eyes

Sit back and play with my soul

Pave hell with silk

Love is an unknown myth

You as consciousness can't be perceived

Love is to be vision or believe

Not in the things that trap the mind

But however,

In our relation to how we spend our time

Either forever

Or for always

Until our dying days

Ervin Nubian Holloway

JUST WORDS

Scattered lyrics

Plastic dreams

Breathless spirit

Each musical note

Are just words I wrote

In order to try a technique in which an attempt is made

To unconsciously control the way my crying vision behave

But the nutrients in my eyes and arms

Aren't available in tearful form

A LOVING HEART

A loving heart beats forever

But it takes more than love

To hold love together

So dreams your dreams

For you can never be sure about everything

Just as long as you're sure about some of the things

Ervin Nubian Holloway

READING POETRY TO A SETTING SUN

Reading poetry to a setting sun

Night knows nothing of my existence

I have painted the universe black with the color of my skin

I am the offspring of my own ideas

Born…

Reincarnated

And spiritually liberated

Who has come to exert inescapable or coercive pressure on the world?

Through the sum of my physical equation

Plant my eyes beneath the soil

And if tears happen to grow

Please know

I'm only crying to create change

Reading poetry to a setting sun

Today I stand to incite a culture revolution

That is an end onto itself

Loving You and Loosing Me!

Spoken to resurrect you in life or death

Through black love and painted pictures

Behind Quranic, biblical and poetic scriptures

And although my soul maybe religiously bankrupted

My present condition remains a constant struggle

Plant my eyes beneath the soil

And if tears happen to grow

Please know

I'm only crying to create change.

HOW?

How dark my days was

How uncontrolled my life was

How convincing the heavens above

How empty my heart was

But how come

How come you never notice these things?

DYING INSIDE

An undug grave

Could it symbolize I'm dying inside

Archaic beliefs

I am poetry in grief

Mourning for the day to worship you

Because from the beginning of God's existence

I prayed to you

Hoping you would hear

To a voice that was calling you near

When you didn't answer

I start-it speaking in tongues

To give rise to optical properties

And dying related philosophies

An undug grave

Could it symbolize I'm dying inside

Ervin Nubian Holloway

SHADES OF LOVE

As I regain consciousness

I'm envy of my own existence

So I write your name inside the color of my dreams

To cure me of this painful awareness

Shades of love

Is the outbreak or the epidemic of my emotions

My "now" is my pain

Missing pages of the color of your skin

Black holes

Everything has been sucked in

I'm doubting much since our departure

But love is at the top of my list

Shades of love is envious

Written words have proven this

Shades of love

Loving You and Loosing Me!

Is the outbreak or the epidemic of my emotions?

Shadows are cast

Today I ask

You to manufacture

My love to produce a different result

Shades of love

Is the outbreak or the epidemic of my emotions?

Ervin Nubian Holloway

DENIAL OF A REVEALED TRUTH

Origin unknown

I never search for someone so hard before

I want you more and more

Deliberate distortions of a past reality

Promises of future trouble

Animating through

A place of ruthless struggle

The cause of my present conditions

Falsehoods are cruel inventions

A denial of a revealed truth

Love has no actual proof

Beside that of emotional attachment

And physical reactment

I rest

No longer need any proof

To prove

The denial of a revealed truth

LET ME CRY FIRST

Let me cry first

I only have tears to quench your thirst

I am an emotional atmosphere

Capable of producing rain

Yet, through all the hardship and pain

My physical form is vaguely sensed

Let me cry first to ease your hurt

From a world that haters tried to leave in ruins

I know what they're doing

But we will brush those haters off

And tell them to get lost

For love only has room to love

And not room to judge

Or room for mistakes

But if this be the case

Then why do haters hate

CHAINED BY CIRCUMSTANCES

Hustling to get by

Anything for you and I

But we often sow what we reap

These streets

Lord knows in those streets

The choices I made were govern by the value

I placed of material things

As oppose to the value I placed on our dreams

Now in the face of my difficulties

I pray your commitment to stay by my side

Will be your commitment to keep me alive

In a world where danger rules

And love chose

To hustle to get by

This why

I am chained by circumstances

WORDS MADE FLESH?

Words made flesh?

I will write your name in parables

Translate your beauty into quantum physics

Decipher your dreams into hieroglyphics

Utter your diary in vain

Sign language maybe use to translate your name

Fill your tub with words

Vocabularies and loving ambitions

Loneliness has a way of reminding me there's a part of me that's missing

Someone special who is hopeless waiting

Through verbal communicating

To guide me from my stage of loneliness

And into

Words made flesh...John Chapter 1 Verse 1-5

YOUR BIRTHMARK

Your birthmark

Contaminates my soul

My pen

My body

My paper

My mind

My heart

Your birthmark

Contaminates

My spirit

Barricades my feelings

My eyes

My dreams

My possibilities

My art

Your birthmark

Contaminates

My love

Loving You and Loosing Me!

My hopes

My life

My emptiness

My beginning

My start

Your birthmark

Contaminates

My breath

My hands

My world

My joy

My smile

My persistence

In a way that punctuates my existence

FOR NOW

When things seem not to go their best

And your life seem a mess

Just remember all days want be good

And things don't work themselves out like you wish they should

But one day it all would make perfect sense in this world of illusion

So for now

Laugh at the confusion

Smile through the tears

Never give up the fight

And keep reminding yourself

That everything will be alright

ORGANIC EYES

Organic eyes

Purged through silence

Support this large vessel

That seems to sail on watery eyes

In time everything dies

Including love

Leaving my "eyes" in complete chaos

As if my tears has somehow been shredded

Nothing is connected

Everything has been separated and embedded

Permanently dismantle

The world my eyes have envision has ended

21 percent of the atmosphere has turned to death and mistrust

My earthly remains are now compound to dust

The only thing is left and disguise

Are...

Organic eyes

WHERE

Where poetry is fed

Where words fall asleep

Where poems speak

Where printed letters sings

Where paper dreams

Where thoughts run oxygen everywhere

Breathe with your eyes

And vision me there

MORNING ROSE

My dripping thoughts

Pierce by your beauty

Causing the seeds to blossom into flowers

When it grows

It becomes the morning rose

Smelling fresh

Sprouting from its earthly nest

It is giving as a dedication of love and heaven

Or something thoughtful and pleasant

And sometimes for season memories and soft blessing

But as I look upon the morning rose

That can not quite match your loveliness

I wonder

How something so beautiful and harmless

Scented and delicate

Can grow something so deadly

As thorns on it

Ervin Nubian Holloway

STIMULATION

A thousand mornings

I hope to wake up and see you smile

So you can place your nectar on my lips

And tell me to take a sip

From a cup of love

Fill with your sexual liquid

Having a penetrating effect

Leaving my mind drowsy and wet

With shelter love and secrets hidden

Naked words and things forbidden

That will give added help to yesterday heart

Clothing the written words of my fleshly parts

So you will know as you mentally undress

That this poem is to stimulate the mind frame monogamist

And not to cause sexual interest

PHYSICAL SENSES

Undress my mind

Drink from my eyes

Taste my laughter

Bless my dreams

Turn me over

And fill me with promises

Pour oil over my spirit

Race your fingers across my lips

Escape between the corners of my mouth

Then breathe inside of me

And make love to me

By means

Other than the physical senses

Ervin Nubian Holloway

THE WIND ASKED ABOUT YOU

Born from the soul of spiritual love

In tune with the dreams that leak from your smile

The sound of your laughter

Can be heard across a million miles

Vibrating between the sheets of bless time

While a glass of filled love

Pours freely from my mind

Giving birth to angels and streams

Yesterday moments

And wishful dreams

Joyful words

And spiritual growth

Giving life to this sexual state

Through sound and hope

The wind asked about you

Time gave me your name

Loving You and Loosing Me!

Memories of a thousand seasons

The gift of lovely things

Winter falls beneath summer and spring

Clothing the nude sky with the thoughts you bring

On the day we first met

At a moment in my life

I will never forget

LOVE

Love controls my thoughts

Love controls my faults

Love control my ideas

Love control my fears

Love has so many ways of controlling me

Taking hold of me

That am constantly falling in love with love

Love controls my heart

Love controls my reason to never be apart

Love controls my dreams

Love controls my everything

Love has so many ways of controlling me

Taking hold of me

That am constantly falling in love with love

Love controls my reality

Love controls me unquestionably

Loving You and Loosing Me!

Love controls my will

Love controls what I feel

Love has so many ways of controlling me

Taking hold of me

Now it's my time to give to love

What love gave to me

A drop of joy

A spoon of emotions

And a cup of eternity

Ervin Nubian Holloway

ARMAGEDDON

Apocalyptic and incarcerated heart

Although we're so close

It feels like we're worlds apart

Armageddon

My world has now come to an end

No life no air no oxygen

How can I breathe without you?

All I can do is think about you

But nothing has been planted where this heart use to be

Don't you know love is best serve when-it blossom for the world to see

So come and share the Garden of Eden with me

And I will give you life for all eternity

LOVING YOU IS SPIRITUAL

The pronunciation of your name

Has me praying toward you

As oppose to

Praying toward heaven

Therefore, it is my belief

To shroud you with faith

That we both may share and keep safe

Those things which are eternal to God

ONLY ME

So many lives I lived with you

Deja'vu

Reincarnated a thousand times

When you were mines

Once before

You will still be mines forever more

Can't imagine my life without you in it

From start to finish

I knew we were meant to be

When time brought together you

And chance brought together me

I am truly blessed

As night comes and the sun set

The moon celebrates its moment in the sky

The moon disappears so a star can appear for you and I

Now the signs in heaven I can clearly see

If there is only you

Then there can be

Only me

SEX VS YOUR INTELLECT

Sex versus your intellect

I prefer your intelligence

Sexual intimacy is irrelevant

Mentally I release sub-atomic particles into your sacredness

Thus I become your first

The eclipse of my body impregnate your universe

Our sex become a nuclear explosion

Passionate, yet radiant energy, is exploding

While pleasure of quantum theory screams from your voice

Perhaps an adequate approach to mental intercourse

Causing my thoughts and me

To melt irresponsibly

ITS VERY JULY

Spring is gone

We wed in June

Love ends too soon

Did love end

Because I couldn't properly love you

Or could it be

Love is an unfortunate accident

Causing my heart to beat rapidly

On a collision which escape becomes a difficulty.

TEACH ME

Teach me to be you

Because I believe a man capacity for change

Is when a woman gives her advice

So warn me against my faults and oversights

For a woman's advice often stress

The fruit and value of what a man need to learn

And the man she grown to love

Becomes her only concern

Her concerns give her the ability of view points and opinions

She consider herself unique and special from other women

She isn't materialistic

With things that are simplistic

She knows that true gifts can only come from the heart

Gifts other consider small

Like flowers and walks in the park

She makes the right choices and this shows intelligence

She is the sense of all form of excellence

She is an angle from above

The kind of woman that would make God fall in love

A woman who my whole life is dedicated to

And I'm proud to say that woman is you.

I ROSE

I rose to see the beauty of Kemet

The land of my birth

The land of twice bless

There I saw Zaire with Auset

The goddess of life

With the moon sleeping in her arms

In order to guide me through the night and keep me from harm

So I could soak in the quietness she shown

To feel a touch of silence I've always known

Through love peace and rest

Culture memories and happiness

That makes the seed of love grow to full blown

That make me beg

To soak in the quietness she shown.

LET ME WALK THROUGH YOUR EYES

What do you see in me

That I don't see

Do you see a misguided mind?

That seems to drink and digest time

Or do you see that I'm intellectual

Clothe inside your eyes

Covered with something special

Let me walk through your eyes

So I can see

How you envision me

Just one glance

And you're able to place me under a trance

Where love exceed the days absorbed

Give to me what I've been dying for

And I will throw away my faith in God who is true

Just to vow all that I am to you

Ervin Nubian Holloway

Let me walk through your eyes

So I can see

How you envision me.

Ervin Nubian Holloway

DO YOU KNOW LOVE

Do you know love?

Do you understand love?

Do you sense love's presence?

Do you want love?

How desperately do you need love?

Do you misrepresent love?

Do you mimic love?

Do you hold on to love?

Do you alter love?

How desperately do you need love?

Do you conceal love?

Do you televise love?

Do you crave for love?

Do you embrace love?

How desperately do you need love?

Do you give love?

Do you accommodate love?

Do you entirely serve love?

Do you shelter love?

How desperately do you need love?

Do you wish for love?

Do you protect love?

Do you yearn for love?

Do you believe in love?

But how desperately do you need love?

A CONTEST BETWEEN RIVALS

Who authorized my eyes to cry?

My heart is tired of saying good-bye

My capacity to function has diminish

I would compete with my soul but my heart has limits

A contest between rivals

Overwhelming evidence depicted in bibles

I am gradually fading away into my own mental and spiritual anguish

Love is spoken in a symbolic language

Beyond what mere words can say

OCCUPATION

What emotional occupation

Has her disagreeing with my disagreements

Whereas her heart seek unemployment

I acknowledge we share the same problems

But love has a way of appearing

In an unexpected or supernatural way

Ervin Nubian Holloway

WE NEED ROOM TO GROW

Can two things

Or two people

And two dreams

Occupy the same space of mind

All at the same time

The possibility is there

If your feminine or omnipresent is every where

But my emotions are closing in on us

Suffocating we

Suffocating me

To let go

Maybe we need room to grow

Ervin Nubian Holloway

LOVE IS NOT A SHORT TERM LOAN

Love is not a short term loan

That consistently brings distress, agitation and everything wrong

It is conduct, expression and taste

A protective representation of somewhere safe

That isn't capable of being overcome or subdued

By opinions, impulses or ever changing views

Love is experimentation

Subject to criticism and pathological investigation

Love makes me so weak

I never met a force so strong

That consistently brings distress, agitation and everything wrong

ECLIPSE

It's like covering the moon

In its different phases

In its different stages

It's like open heart surgery

The feeling of my own eclipse thumping

1 Beat

2 Beat

My heart is pumping

Damn she's so intoxicating

I'm contemplating

Whether I should say hello

GLOBAL WARMING

Imminent examination

Preoccupied with my own preoccupation

The pain I hide

Have me paralysis

Where it's raining inside

E'F-5s may form

Numerous reports of my emotional thunderstorms

Causing strong winds of pain and hurt

The national weather service has issued an alert

That flooding is the act of me crying

Armageddon, could it be my world is dying

Beep…this is a warning

The cause of global warming

Ervin Nubian Holloway

I DECLINE

I decline to tell the world how I carried gravity

I decline to tell the world how in my life you create so much confusion

I decline to tell the world what they see on the surface is only an illusion

I decline to tell the world how you have a cure to a virus call love

I decline to tell the world how there's no life or love after death

I decline to tell the world what feelings for you I have left

I decline to tell the world how I cultivate your smile

I decline to tell the world how I distribute your eyes

I decline to tell the world what constitute not 1 not 2 but a thousand tries

I decline to tell the world how you use DNA to make me in the image of God

I decline to tell the world how I dissolved into liquid matter

I decline to tell the world what makes tears shatter

I decline to tell the world how you got me battling with eternal forces

I decline to tell the world how you are so demanding

I decline to tell the world what we need is understanding

Regardless what the earth shares between man and woman - boy and girl

I will always decline to share you with the world

172

SOLAR WIND

Paint the air uninterruptly and spiritually

Let me sin and not be forgiven

I am an organism who is biodegradable with the living

Whereas I sometimes correspond with my own breathing

To use CPR in a hurry

For the use of bypass surgery

Because bypass surgery doesn't always work

Because it hurts

To truly know in the end

That love will be blown by solar wind

COMMERCIAL DRUG -VS- EMOTIONAL HIGH

Let's get high

Elevate our consciousness

Without the use of illegal substance

We are a point in time

Traveling from point "a" to cloud "9"

Now exhale for me

A kilo gram of TLC (tender - loving - care)

With you being my greatest addiction

It's hard for me to fight this affliction

Nevertheless,

I don't need the photographic techniques of rehab

Nor the use of marijuana to make me smile or laugh

When all I need is that you save for me

The joy and happiness you've always gave to me

Ervin Nubian Holloway

CLOSED DOORS

Ice skating across sheets of frozen tears

Her emotions are mine humble beginnings

Sleep walking on pages of happy endings

Where never endings always ends

And friends

Pretend to be friends

Through a flurry of inactivity

Biological warfare,

Social mishaps and misery

So if I can

I will erase the suffering by purchasing love at pharmaceutical drug stores

Love can sometimes be vertical

Even behind closed doors.

WORLD WAR 3

Arm hostile conflict and combat

My feelings are planning against an emotional attack

From pain, suffering, physical discomfort and mental abuse

Are all weapons of mass destruction that you've used

Does this prove you don't love me - you don't care

Or is it another form of your brutal warfare

Knowing there's nothing to shield

Me from an emotional battlefield

Or to combat

An emotional attack

That has left this soldier to choose

Between pain, suffering, physical discomfort and mental abuse.

UNEXPECTED DIFFERCULTY

Survival,

A cliff

Survival,

A myth

Survival,

A condemned soul

Survival,

Morse code

Survival is a right

To fight

For love at all times

If so

Then why am I constantly looking for a life line

SUN BURNED

Subpoena my smile

I just wanna make you happy

Even without your presence

I continue to feel your absence

But shit always happens

Because I thought I would evolve and graduate into a higher being

But the rising and setting of the sun brings

The disunite

Of darkness and light

Brilliantly causing sunburns

Ervin Nubian Holloway

BIOLOGICAL CLOCK

Biological clock

Predates my here

Predates my now

As to why a living organism like love should be genetically engineered

I leave my finger prints at the edge of your soul

As I hang on a cliff ready to spiritually die

But if I jump would you save what you and I

Have genetically engineered

Biological clock

Predates my here

Predates my now

As to why a living organism like love should be genetically engineered

Chemical compounds within a living heart

The toxic sustenance of love and deception

Love is a form of emotional terrorism involving a biological weapon

Loving You and Loosing Me!

That I have genetically engineered

Biological clock

Predates my here

Predates my now

As to why a living organism like love should be genetically engineered

The clock on my wall is either dying or ill

If I could rewind the moment when time stood still

I would celebrate every second, every minute, every hour

Telling the world how much I love you.

RADIOACTIVE

I can explode at any time

Entirely consumed and exonerate your mind

Allow you to invest in capital nourishment

Digesting economic intelligence is worthless

If used for the wrong purpose

Like inducing fertilizer into the soil from which I was created

Branches of my gynecological tree x-rated

Has became a growing resistance

Society seem content even though children go missing

In a neighborhood of numerical difference

Maybe I should take justice in my own hand

If law enforcement want take the stand

To save children from the dictates of Amber's alert

Why should a mother give birth

If the system don't work

By becoming psychological passive

I can explode at any time

Radioactive.

HIBERNATION

As I begin to hibernate inside you

Our love becomes domesticated

For time unknown I have waited

To electronically replace the mechanics of love

Our love becomes domesticated

There's no anesthesia for my emotions to be compensated

Especially when I worked so hard to avoid

The financial responsibilities of a broken heart

In exchange for an early retirement.

For time unknown I have waited

And softly contemplated

The toxic fabric of undressing the atoms in love

But I'm not prepared for Armageddon

Because love is a nuclear reactor.

To electronically replaced the mechanics of love

Ervin Nubian Holloway

Requires me to be emotionally illiterate

And religiously inconsiderate

To the point where I enjoy the indescribable sins of love

That I'm prepared to go to hell for.

SLOPPY SECONDS

Want soooo bad to place you in a time capsule

Temporarily to suspend my social circumstances

Bacteria contaminate your wounds

Politicians contaminates your hopes and trust

Implication of scattered disgust

Written matter illustrated

My actual existing needs evaluated

For I am influenced by organized commercialism

Agricultural products and prisons

Subject to harmful influences

Thanks to the wealthy, Americans lives are in ruins

Purchases of redeemable premiums are permanent

Photographic images of college loans are fraudulent

Nonetheless,

They can kiss my azz

I don't need the sloppy second of the upper-class

Want sooo bad to place you in a time capsule

Temporarily to suspend my social circumstances.

When the eyes aren't available

Tears become unavoidable

Resulting in

Various scorched appearance

Leaving the eyes stain

The pupil drain

And the world against you.

LIQUID

Am I allergic to angels?

Assure me

That heaven will cure me

Before loneliness causes me to evaporate

I overstand that we both need an environment where we may drink and flourish

But you say don't rush love - be patient - don't hurry

How long do I have to wait?

And how long will it take

To quench this thirst that I have for you

I honestly make this path for you

Through oceans

Seas

Ponds

Ice

Steam

Whether I'm sipping H_2O

Waterfalls

Rain

Ervin Nubian Holloway

Thunder storms

Sprinkles or springs

Whether I'm throwing pennies in wishing wells

Lakes

Waterways

Rivers or springs

Or dripping wet in all thee above

It matters little

As long as you drown me with your love.

POETRY IN MOTION

My eyes are poetic visions

My lips are poetic words

My dreams sleep poetically

My hands paint poetic pictures

My prayers are poetic scriptures

My lungs breathes in poetic oxygen

My ears hear poetic music

My taste comes in 7 poetic flavors

My heart beats to a poetic pace

My arms want to carry you to a poetic place

My thoughts are a poetilness of gather consciousness

My past lives are a product of my poetic reincarnation

My oneness wants us to share in a vastness of poetic union

And me,

I am poetry in motion

Because I'm poetically in love with you

PSYCH

Her love is psych

I sense that she sense me

She knows my every thought

I lay in my bed thinking…that she's thinking of me

But she has a psych block

I stone wall with graffiti written all over it

The only thing she leaves behind is a painted heart

Beating like an African drum

Leading me…

Into a melody

Of psych paradise

ORGANIC

There is a cause and effect to love

Residential, pigmented in a thousand chapters

Fictional and non-fictional in a happily ever after

There is a cause and effect to love

Uncompromising, abstinate, concern

Unmovable, strong, firm

Converting cosmic growth

Into an organic compound of love and hope.

Ervin Nubian Holloway

WATER POURED OVER LOVE

You are my religion

My baptism

Who has bestowed upon me

Light and decision to correct

Both close and distance vision

Through the promising of wishing

Occurring every second

Through the womb of existence

Where spells are cast

To ensure our love will last

God and the clouds above

Water poured over love

Water

Water poured over love

Not cable of existence

Unacceptable in dying need

191

Loving You and Loosing Me!

I find it difficult to breathe

My eyes have been rape

I'm consider something of a mistake

Without substance or sense

Too loving to be of any significant

Can't find peace or rest

Traveling on the road to my unhappiness

Water poured over love

Water

Water poured over love.

If they ask me why I love you

I will give them a million reasons

If they ask me who am I

I will tell them I'm you

If they ask me

Is that that the sun in the sky

I will tell them

No!

That is your smile

If they ask me who is more important

You or God

I will tell them you

If they ask me

Let's go search for diamonds and gold beyond measure

I will tell them why

When I have already found my treasure

If they ask me

Is there nothing I wouldn't do

I will happily tell them

I'll even sell my soul to the devil

Just for you

Water poured over love

Water

Water poured over love

Loving You and Loosing Me!

Water poured over love

Water

Water poured over love.

A HEALTHY RELATIONSHIP

A working relationship works best

When it is free from stress

Happiness can be a substitute for sadness through nutritional intake

And using vitamins can be good for any calorie heart brake

For vitamin-C is recommended when only one person

A

R

E

S

Vitamin-A is recommended when only one person is receiving

T

T

E

N

T

I

O

N

Loving You and Loosing Me!

Vitamin-D is recommended if either person fail to dream their

R

E

A

M

S

Vitamin-E is recommended if

T

E

R

N

I

T

Y

Is eternally running out of time.

CONSEQUENCES OF A DICTIONARY

Domino theory - noun: the theory that if one act or event is allowed to take place a series of similar acts or events will follow or be trace.

If this theory is true

How do me and you

Co-habitat

Through a series of similar acts or events that determine our fate.

ARE YOU

Are you aware

Identifiable,

Develop,

Reliable,

Biochemical

Improve,

Memorable,

Prevailing

Artistic,

Perceivable,

Realistic,

Nurturing

Providing,

Strong,

Undividing,

Creative

Architectural

Evolve,

Sexual,

Metric

Pleasured

Priceless

Treasured

Or please just tell me

Are you conceptual

Distinguished by some unusual quality that is intellectual.

Ervin Nubian Holloway

ZERO - 69

I can smell your perfume

Let's migrate to the moon

Register your name

On the surface of the Martian plane

Place the universe in the palm of your hand

And use heaven as a platform so you can stand

Travel at light speed through space and time

61

63

65

67

69

LOVE SICK

If a vaccine is needed only

Then my immune system can't keep me from being lonely

For I may be immune to a cold

Virus or a flu

Or even…what you're putting me through

Maybe I'm simply love sick or lazy

Lately I've been coughing, sneezing because I miss you like crazy

My health is fading

I desperately need saving

Although heaven has been critical

Let me awake in your arms and not in a hospital

Because if I rest

I rest with you through eternity

If I die

I die with you eternally

SLEEPLESS

I had a dream

But I felled asleep dreaming it away

You said that I will be ok

That night time will repeat itself repeatedly

Immediately,

Sleep begin to patronize me

Without regard to my resting needs

As if I was a spinal disease

CONTACT

Make contact with me

Touch my thoughts

Know me

Like you never known any man before

Because I can be all that you want and more

Your lover

Your husband

Your dreams

Your soul

Your spirit

Your after life

Your Alpha - Omega and friend

Even like Christ

To die for your sins

HIDE AND SEEK

Immature in all my ideas

Peer pressure

Or pressure by my peers

I would schedule love and interview

But knowing you

You might piss me the "f" off

In which I will classify as a lost

In this game of hide and seek

Ervin Nubian Holloway

WINTER SOLSTICE

Keep me warm

This room is empty

That my emptiness is even empty

Don't tempt me

Because it snows sometimes in my bed

Whereas freezing and sleepless thoughts of you are frozen in my head

Is this an Antarctic celestial river

My body shivers

Under complicated matters

And your cold heart isn't making it any better

For my emotions are not adopted to conditions at 32 below

Or 27 days, 7 hours, 45 minutes, 11.5 seconds of snow

Winter solstice

Glaciers are likely to form

Ice that pierces the heart can cause harm

There's no expiration date on arctic love

Loving You and Loosing Me!

Sleet - hail and feelings of affection fall from above

Heaven and nature releases its own DNA into space

Winter solstice has become human and hereditary

Making a lonely heart such a cold place.

Ervin Nubian Holloway

SOLAR POWER

At some future time

The heavens will be mine

And I will build you a shrine

An altar

A tower

Without the means of solar power

In the event that stars are edit for editorial purposes

At some future time

When moments and nights forget to surface

SOLAR SYSTEM

You know

There isn't enough space in the universe

To separate me from you

Though my feelings are stars in a geometrical figure

I will use fractions

Multiplication and subtractions

To divide anti-matter and dark matter

To make your world better

And use hyphens and black holes to bridge this universal space

Which separates us by time - distant and place

Despite the fact you are a Pisces on the constellation map

I look forward to the zodiac south of Andromeda to bridge our gap

SOLAR RADIATION

Solar radiation

Radiate your radiant beauty

So much so

I tend to hide in attics

And write objectionable poetry that is dramatic

Filled with nouns, adverbs, propositions and verbs

Preferably for you as a dialect for sweet words

Even to the point of catching a cavity or tooth decay

Since solar radiation

Radiate your radiant beauty

I hope it never goes away

SOLAR ECLIPSE

You considered what's next for us

I have to considered what's best for us

We can't depend on celestial objects to determine our fate

When emotional weight

Is measured by the earth's course in relation to our heart path

Either after the sun set

Or during its aftermath

SOLAR FLARE

A solar flare

Couldn't compare

To the sudden outburst of energy

That the spark from your smile

Does and do light up the world

Pi

I try to illustrate

A visual creation

In relation

To what I could graphically describe in decimals

How the unit of length to measure forever

Could bring our relationship closer together

Near a transcendental number

Three point one

Four - one

Five - nine - two

Six - five

That would keep our love alive.

DOMINO EFFECT

What it is

What you've done to me

No woman ever has

And though I was willing to make it last

You masqueraded as if my willingness was useless acronyms

Materially fashion in a dictionary of celestial gems

Where promises you promise

Are never promised

No matter how much I try to pay homage

I know that if the theory of one act or event

Is allowed to take place or proceed farther

A series of similar acts or events follow

Ervin Nubian Holloway

CHOCOLATE SEIZURE

Hey chocolate

I think your complexion is spiritual

So lyrical

That I'm seeminglessly and endlessly

Thinking I'm the word of God made manifest

But I confess

That chocolate taste sweeter when it melts between parallel planes

And I could never interrupt your beauty or change

The physical manifestation of sensory convulsion that claim

To be the cause of an abnormal electrical discharge in the brain

FROM BOTTLED *W*ATER TO BOTTLE TEARS

To avoid the unavoidable

My tears are various form of carbohydrate

Where hydrogen and oxygen mate

To impregnate

The element of water in its three states

Liquid,

Solid,

And gas that evaporates

Manufacture for preparation

As an item sold in stores for liquidation

Cash only

Emotional company is invalid

Loneliness can be such an incompetent tragic

In the mist of so many passing years

I went from bottle water

To bottle tears

CALL ME

Call me sometime

Communicate freely with my mind

Our conversations doesn't always have to be cosmetic

Nor cosmological

It can be a force that resist

That pulls

That is unstoppable

That is possible

It can be a reservoir of natural influences

That doesn't offer leniency to an unloving endurance

It can be anything you want it to be

As long as you call me.

WHEN YOU BREATHE

Element, metallic, priceless gold plated breath

When you breathe

Make me into a breathing material

From which atomic energy can produce love

Insert Oxygen into my annoyance

My disappointments,

My disbeliefs

Before love gets the chance to evaporate

And deteriorate

Into hydrogen and synthetic grief

When the earth leaves me in space and mate with the universe

Save me from artificial respiration

During my time of emotional strangulation

Ervin Nubian Holloway

SKELETONS IN HER CLOSET

Widespread confusion

Abundance of illusions

Naked suggestions

Sinfully barbaric,

The core of primitive confessions

Endless combatants and fraudulent practices

Are frequently use as medieval tactics

Skeletons in Zaire's closet

No longer are my tears made of flesh

For the bones and my optic nerves are the only clue I leave behind

She slams the door

I checked to see it is closed

I peer in the key hole

Secretly I cry in the dark

Castrated before my sexual maturity

The conditions of my illegitimate birthmark

Loving You and Loosing Me!

Has a way of transforming my y-chromosome into a grotesque bastard

Making me aggressive, selfish and sometimes, unlawfully hazardous

To learn from my lesson

And to cool my aggression

What door should I choose?

Door number #1

Door number #2

I choose door number #3, secretly

I cry in the dark because no one knows it's me

Ervin Nubian Holloway

WHAT I WOULDN'T DO

I will subdue you with the gender of my words

Tell you things that God never heard

Restore unto you a love that is true

Wash away your tears that I may know how to comfort you

Do the things that no one has done

Bring you the moon

The stars

And the sun

So you may know

You are my prayer

My heaven in which only me and you can share

I'M ME

Maybe I don't meet your expectations

But congratulations

I'm me

Maybe I don't meet your standards

Guess what, it's something I can handle

But I'm me

Maybe I don't meet your faith and dreams

So what, God still provides me with everything

And I'm still me

Maybe I don't meet your desire of a pretty girlfriend

Guess what, beauty lives within

And I'm me

Maybe I don't have the body of a diva

Guess what, I'm not the only one either

But I'm me

Maybe I don't meet your type with the

Overwhelming craving

The naughty misbehaving

Ervin Nubian Holloway

The unmovable style

The illuminating smile

The photographic eyes

The soft good-byes

The irresistible skin tone

The hair that is naturally long

But guess what, I'm me

The symbolic imagine of black womanhood

YOU ARE

You are my sunken treasure

That caused the ocean to smile and make a wish

A treasure God would drown for

And a woman he would love to be with

You're my inspiration of light

That consumes my darkness that grows

And the river in the mist of my lonely eyes

That flows and flows

You are the reason why I live

And the manifestation of my soul

The missing reason why

Me and God were half complete

Until you made us brighter, happy and whole

Ervin Nubian Holloway

MY ANGEL

Soak my mind within the heaven clouds

And start drinking

What it is that I'm thinking?

Then drink constantly

Into the thoughts of you

That bathe inside of me.

WHERE

Where poetry is fed

Where words fall asleep

Where poems speak

Where printed letters sings

Where paper dreams

Where my running thought

Run water everywhere

Meditate with your eyes

And vision me there

Ervin Nubian Holloway

FROM THE TASTE OF YOUR WET BEAUTY

When beauty cross over

And try to walk sober

I'll be drunk off your loveliness

Like poured wine

That seem to stagger time

I could never thirst

From the taste of your wet beauty

Let me paint your water bed

Do your understand what is being said

Let me break it down to you instead

Your beauty is like a river

That is rushing through my head

I could never thirst

From the taste of your wet beauty

Loving You and Loosing Me!

Woman you make me stutter

I am intoxicated by your beauty

So let me drink your color

That will produce effects in beauty

Different from those produced by others

227

Ervin Nubian Holloway

TRANSPARENT LOVE

Transparent love

Seems vivid to eyes that are without protection

It is like a stimulant

Causing mental erection

Neurotically, affecting the soil and baring leaves

In an obstructive manner

By withholding the air we breathe

Transparent love

Seems to have an inherited tendency

Through the worship of fostered memories

By a force or action that suppresses love and seasons

Or any toxic relationship or reasons

Transparent love

Is dealing with women with broken hearts in urban poverty

Where tears, mud and mirrors are shaped into pottery

So that the objects and the images of a man

Can be seen thereof

In a woman perspective

As transparent love

Ervin Nubian Holloway

PICK UP A PEN

Pick up a pen

And write your name inside my eyes

And make a wish

Fill my arms with flowers

And I'll make up for the lost hours

When those you love wasn't there

For all the times they didn't care

When needed a shoulder to cry on

For all the people you thought you could rely on

Pick up a pen

For the many times you wanted to say

Why is he acting this way?

He seem to love me so much

When we first touch

But now it seem as if he is distance

He never listens

Oh god, what did I do

Loving You and Loosing Me!

He never hold me the way he use to

How can I be such a fool?

When people are to love

And things are to use

So if this ever happen to you

And you need a friend

Pick up a pen.

LET ME WALK THROUGH YOUR EYES

What do you see in me?

That I don't see

Do you see a misguided mind?

That seems to drink and digest time

Or do you see that I'm intellectual

Drape inside your eyes

Covered with something special

Let me walk through your eyes

So I can see

How you see me

Just one glance

And you're able to place me under a trance

Where love exceeds the days absorbed

So penetrate me and give me what I've been dying for

And I will throw away my faith in God who is true

Just to vow all that I am to you

Let me walk through your eyes

So I can see

How you see me

Ervin Nubian Holloway

About the Author

Ervin Nubian Holloway is from Montgomery, Alabama. He developed his love for writing while spending sixteen years for a federal crime he did not commit. He is also a public speaker, poet, mentor and an advocate for the well-being of children and humanity.

Ervin resides in Montgomery, Alabama.

Made in the USA
Las Vegas, NV
10 November 2021